FROM
PROPHET
TO SON

FROM PROPHET TO SON

Advice of Joseph F. Smith to His Missionary Sons

Compiled and Edited by
HYRUM M. SMITH III
SCOTT G. KENNEY

Deseret Book Company
Salt Lake City, Utah
1981

© 1981 Deseret Book Company
All rights reserved
Printed in the United States of America
First printing November 1981

Library of Congress Cataloging in Publication Data

Smith, Joseph Fielding, 1838-1918.
 From prophet to son.

 Includes index.
 1. Smith, Joseph Fielding, 1838-1918. 2. Mormons—
United States—Correspondence. 3. Church of Jesus Christ
of Latter-day Saints—Missions. I. Smith, Hyrum M.,
1941-   II. Kenney, Scott G., 1946-   . III. Title.
BX8695.S63A35   289.3'3 [B]   81-15173
ISBN 0-87747-885-6   AACR2

Contents

Preface

He was alone, barely sixteen, three thousand miles from home, and penniless. Surviving on a meager diet of sweet potatoes, prickly pears, and poi, he struggled to learn the language that would enable him to preach the gospel to the natives.

He later recalled, "They had different habits to anything I had before known, and their food, and dress and houses and everything were new and strange. Out among these people at once I was sent alone, to study, and learn if possible (for to me at that time it seemed impossible) their language and their characteristics in order that I might labor for their good. For three months this seclusion from the world continued, but the history of that short period of my life never can be told. I had ample time to feel after the Lord and to draw near to him with my whole soul. It seemed to me as tho' I had no friend but God, although the natives were kind and did what they could in *their* way to make me happy. Semi-occasionally I would get a letter from some of the brethren or from home, at the sight of which my heart would swell too big for utterance, and I would almost choke with joy from which I could find no relief but in tears and prayers.

"I had no companion and had to bear my joys and griefs in solitude, conscious of the presence of none but God, and at times, I must confess, it seemed to me that even

He was a long way off. This three months' seclusion was twice interrupted by the presence for a few days each time of R____, suffering with temporary aberration of mind from which but poor consolation was derived.

"When I had mastered the language, I began to move around, from place to place, in the discharge of my duties, and so occasionally met with some of the Elders, and had the pleasure of their society, and once in six months we would meet in conference, when we would let go all holts, open the floodgates of our pent-up feelings and have fairly a roaring cataract of joy! I know what it is to be away from friends, in a foreign land, among the 'heathen' and 'without hope,' almost, for I have been there."

Thus, Joseph F. Smith's initiation into missionary work was a baptism of fire. But he emerged with an unshakable testimony of the restored gospel and The Church of Jesus Christ of Latter-day Saints. Like his patriarch father and prophet uncle, Joseph F. devoted his life to the service of others. After his four-year mission to Hawaii, he returned to the Salt Lake Valley for two years before being sent on a three-year mission to England. Home again for just six months, Joseph F. was called upon to help reestablish the Hawaiian mission, which required most of 1864. He presided over the European Mission from 1874 to 1875, and again in 1877.

Between 1895 and 1914, Joseph F. Smith sent twelve sons on missions. He wrote them hundreds of letters filled with love, counsel, anecdotes, and doctrinal discourses. Through the courtesy of the Church Archives, the editors have had access to Joseph F.'s copies of 334 of those letters, for which we express our appreciation. Additional letters are in the possession of Hyrum M. Smith III.

Extracts for this compilation were made on the basis of their relevance to modern missionaries, insight into the development of strong religious character, and glimpses into the father-son relationships of this prophetic family.

Joseph F. Smith often said of his family, "They are all

the wealth I have." And to one of his sons he wrote, "When I have passed beyond, I would live in my children, if I could, and although generations may come and go, not one shall be so distant or remote that my interest shall cease in them." So, it is to the descendents of Joseph F. Smith, and missionaries everywhere, that this book is dedicated.

Introduction:
Missionary Experiences
of Joseph F. Smith

Early Life
(1838-54)

Joseph F. Smith was only five when his father Hyrum and uncle Joseph were killed at Carthage Jail. His memory of his father was general and impressionistic—a tall, powerfully built man commanding the love and respect of his people; a man of great energy and undying loyalty to his brother and the cause they died for. One memory was indelibly impressed on young Joseph F.: two bodies stretched out in the Mansion House at Nauvoo, Joseph shot in the chest, lower abdomen, and back; Hyrum, in the face, at close range.

Recollections of his mother, Mary Fielding Smith, were more intimate and detailed—the journey across Iowa, the hardships of Winter Quarters, and the three-and-a-half-month trek to the Salt Lake Valley. They arrived in late September 1848, and spent the winter in their wagons— Mary, Joseph F., and his sister Martha Ann, and the children of Hyrum and his deceased wife Jerusha—John, Jerusha, and Sarah. In the spring, the family cleared some land in the foothills, planted grain and potatoes, and began construction of a two-room adobe house. Joseph F. was the herd boy, caring for the livestock that provided milk, meat, and eggs. Crickets devoured most of their first crops, but still it appeared that after years of persecution and tragedy, the family might look forward to peace, if not immediate prosperity. Then, in the summer of 1852, Mary came down with a severe cold. Years of hardship and deprivation proved too great for her. In late September, Joseph F. became an orphan.

At the news of his mother's death, Joseph F. fainted and for some time afterward appeared to be in a state of shock. Through all the trials they had passed, Mary had been the stabilizing force in his life. Joseph F. often referred to her as "my sainted mother," the epitome of true motherhood. To his wife Alice, Joseph F. once wrote, "O! my God, how I love and cherish true Motherhood! Nothing beneath the celestial kingdom can surpass my deathless love for the sweet, true, noble soul who gave me birth. My *own, own* Mother. O! she was good! She was true! She was indeed a Saint! A royal daughter of God! To her I owe my very existence, as also my success in life, coupled with the favor and mercy of God."

Through example, Mary Fielding instilled in Joseph F. the traits that would characterize his entire life—hard work, self-reliance, devotion to duty, and, above all, loyalty to family and church.

Ironically, it may have been Joseph F.'s sense of family responsibility, coupled with the quick temper of his youth, that led indirectly to his first mission call. One day at school, Joseph F.'s younger sister was about to be physically punished by her teacher. When Joseph F. intervened, the teacher came after him, whereupon Joseph F. administered the teacher a sound thrashing and got himself expelled from school. Church authorities sensed that Joseph F. needed a more constructive outlet for his energies, and Joseph F. was more than willing to prove himself in the mission field.

If one mission aroused the interest of the Saints more than any other during the early 1850s, it was the mission to which Joseph F. was called, the Sandwich Islands (Hawaii). The main body of Saints had barely settled in the Salt Lake

Valley when ten missionaries were called to the islands. They landed at Honolulu December 12, 1850, and the next day, according to George Q. Cannon, "we ascended a mountain in the vicinity of the town and erected a small altar of stones, and then bowed ourselves in prayer before the Lord, dedicating those lands to him."

The British and American residents of Honolulu were indifferent to the message the missionaries brought, however, and within three months the mission president and four missionaries had left for other fields or returned home. Five remained, determined to learn the native tongue and deliver their message to the Hawaiian people. Their perseverance was rewarded. Within seven months, George Q. Cannon and his companion had baptized two hundred on Maui alone, and by the spring of 1854 word reached Utah that "upwards of 4000" natives had joined the Church. Just nine days before Joseph F. left Salt Lake City, the *Deseret News* published extracts of a letter from a missionary on Maui: "Elders are now preaching on all of the islands in the group, and hundreds are flocking to the standard of truth. Over 100 have been baptized on this island since the October conference, and some of the islands have increased at a more rapid rate."

On May 5, 1854, Joseph F. left Salt Lake City and quickly caught up with Brigham Young's party, which had just begun a tour of central and southern Utah. For nearly a year, Ute Indians had attacked Mormon settlements, driving off the livestock and plundering indiscriminately. President Young, with Heber C. Kimball and several of the Twelve, was visiting communities, urging inhabitants to "fort up" and strengthen their defenses. Near Nephi, shortly after Joseph F. joined the company, Chief Walker sent word to Brigham Young that he was sick and wanted him to give him a blessing. President Young blessed the chief and gave him cattle and a wagon of flour and wheat. The next day, at Walker's request, President Young blessed the chief's sick daughter, who immediately recovered.

Declaring the healing to be a miracle, the Indians returned stolen cattle and horses, and President Young's party continued on through Fillmore to Cedar City.

On May 21, under the supervision of Parley P. Pratt, Joseph F. and the other twenty-one missionaries destined for the islands left the Young party at Cedar City and struck out for California. Sixteen days later, they arrived at San Bernardino, the southwesternmost colony of the "Mormon Corridor" to the sea. Elder Pratt went directly on to San Francisco to assume his responsibilities as mission president in that city and to arrange passage for the missionaries to Honolulu. Meanwhile, Joseph F. and his companions worked for the Latter-day Saint settlers and sold their wagons and animals to a company of Australian Saints on their way to Zion. Having thus earned their fares, on the Fourth of July the missionaries prevailed upon the San Bernardino Saints to take them to San Pedro, where they boarded a ship for San Francisco.

The increased traffic between the West Coast and Hawaii suggested to mission authorities that the purchase of a sailing vessel might be a good investment. With missionaries en route to and from Hawaii acting as the crew, mission costs could be cut, communication improved, and perhaps some profit made hauling freight. Unfortunately, the ship purchased proved unseaworthy, and the missionaries equally deficient as sailors. The project was quickly abandoned, resulting in the loss of funds earned in San Bernardino. Departure was delayed until September 8, when Joseph F. and eight others were able to sail on board the *Vaquaro*, the others to follow in November.

Honolulu, a city of ten thousand, was teeming with activity. New schools, churches, hospitals, hotels, and government offices were evidence of a boom in foreign trade. Liberty House sold parisols, silk waistcoats, bird cages, window glass, and iron bedsteads. Taverns abounded. Next to the recently opened Honolulu flour mill stood a three-story custom house built of coral, like the royal palace a few blocks away. Nearly four hundred whaling ships arrived in Hawaiian ports annually, and the sugar cane market had grown so quickly that plantation owners imported Chinese workers to make up the labor shortage. Still, nine-tenths of the city's population was native Hawaiian, most living in the traditional thatched huts.

After a week in the capital, Joseph F. and Silas Smith were assigned to Maui, the island where the mission had experienced such rapid growth under George Q. Cannon. As they neared the port of Lahaina, Joseph F. contracted a high fever. As soon as they landed, word spread like wildfire. The natives were well acquainted with diseases brought by white men. Less than a year and a half before, a smallpox epidemic had broken out in Honolulu that eventually killed thousands. The native population was being ravaged by new diseases. Cholera, venereal diseases, smallpox, and leprosy reduced the population from an estimated three hundred thousand in 1778 to less than forty-five thousand a century later.

Joseph F. was taken to the home of Elder Francis A. Hammond to recover. President and Sister Hammond were the only American LDS missionaries on the island at the time. Silas was immediately assigned to Kula, a region near the central part of the island. "I felt for him," President Hammond confided to his diary, "knowing what he has to undergo in preaching and in residing among the people. Brother Joseph is the son of Hyrum Smith, the martyred prophet. He is not yet 16 years old, but bids fain to make a mighty man in this Kingdom."

Recovering quickly from the fever, Joseph F. accompanied President Hammond and an Elder Karren to the neighboring island of Lanai. Hawaiian law forbade native emigration, but a sympathetic chief on Lanai offered the use of his Lanai land as a temporary gathering place for the native Saints until they would be permitted to emigrate to Zion. A colony named the City of Joseph had only recently been started in the center of the island. President Hammond had been given general jurisdiction over the settlement, and Elder Karren the "temporal" affairs. They were gratified to find that the "pioneers" had raised a small native house for the resident missionary, Elder Green; had planted thirty acres of sweet potatoes, corn, beans, and melons; and had laid out two mile-long main streets and two other intersecting streets, following the pattern prescribed by the Prophet Joseph. Elders Hammond, Karren, and Green dedicated the City of Joseph, and, according to one present, "we felt to prophecy that from that place salvation should go forth to this people."

After several days on Lanai, Joseph F. returned with President Hammond to Lahaina, where they remained until beginning a tour of the island on October 23. The following day, they reached Kula and found that Silas had made rapid progress in the language. Joseph F., like Silas, was to be left in Kula to live alone among the natives in order to acquire the language as quickly as possible. Before leaving, President Hammond gave him a blessing:

> The spirit of prophecy and of revelation rested upon me, and great and mighty were the blessings which were pronounced upon his head, even that inasmuch as the Lord had called him to go forth and preach his everlasting gospel, even so he would bear him off triumphant, and a great work should he accomplish on these lands; that his mind should expand, his intellectual power should enlarge, and a mighty man in council should he be, and the spirit of his father Hyrum the martyr should rest upon him.

Before these prophecies were fulfilled, however, Joseph F. was to pass through severe trials. He was able to acquire the language quickly, but, as one of his fellow missionaries noted,

When the gospel was first introduced upon these lands, the people were baptized by scores and hundreds. The elders could hardly walk out into the street but what they would find somebody who wished to be baptized. Such is not the case at the present time. The principal labors of the elders now seem to be to feel after those who have already been baptized, to strengthen them, and to instruct them in their temporal as well as spiritual salvation.

As for temporal conditions, Maui was far from the paradise island now known to travelers. After twenty-one months, Joseph F. wrote:

I have seen many things since I have been on the islands, and some of them are apalling. I have seen whol famelies who ware one sallid wars [?] of scabes (having the itch) and everry stich or rag they had about them or on their premisis, ware alive with the itch. I have slept in these circonstances. I have shaken hands with those whos body and handes ware a scab! I have eaten food mixed up like unto batter with such handes, and I never was so hearty, but I cannot say strong, in my life. . . . I have slept in places where should my hog sleep my stumache would forbid my eating of it. . . . I have slept with my brethren on the same mat with those who wore rotten! and stunk with diseas! and I have seen more than this.

Though the natives were usually willing to share what they had with the missionaries, food was always scarce. It was not at all uncommon to go without food for two or three days at a time, and without any meat for a week or longer. Poi and sweet potatoes were the staples, occasionally enriched with fish, pork, or dog.

7

Receiving no money from home, Joseph F. frequently suffered for adequate clothing, and conferences frequently included pleas for a shirt, a pair of pants, or shoes for the missionaries. On at least one occasion, Joseph F. and his companion were forced to take turns attending meetings because they had only one set of clothes between them.

Equally trying were the spiritual conditions. Protestant missionaries had been working the islands since 1820, and by the arrival of Joseph F., nearly one-third of the population was Christian. He found that members of the Church were considerably influenced by their former ministers:

> Many fear and tremble when they hear the discouraging and mournful tales of destruction which awaits us, as the sectarian priests say, and are continually casting into their faces to try to turn them back to their old path of destruction. I will say that the priests who are here take particular pains to inform those who have come in the Church that they know Joseph Smith to be a thief and a whoremaster and everything else that they can think of. . . . The people are like children; almost any little story will scare them and they are quick to forget the blessings of God, although there are some exceptions.

Nevertheless, in spite of the physical hardship and the tendency of the people to revert to their former traditions, the growth Joseph F. experienced far exceeded the tribulations he suffered, and the love he gained for the Hawaiian people and their love for him bonded them together throughout his life.

Joseph F.'s rapid progress in the language was considered extraordinary. He applied himself diligently, and by Christmas was acknowledged as the most fluent in Hawaiian of the missionaries in his group. When called upon to speak in the local April conference, according to his president, Joseph F. "arose and spoke a few moments by the spirit causing all the saints to rejoice exceedingly. He has only been here six months. The Lord has been with him in getting hold of the language. He spoke very feelingly and I was rejoiced much to hear his voice in the native language."

The missionaries' facility in Hawaiian was crucial, not only for teaching investigators, but also for instructing the members and directing Church functions. George Q. Cannon had returned to San Francisco to begin printing the Book of Mormon in Hawaiian, but during Joseph F.'s mission, very little Church literature was available in the native tongue. Consequently, the Saints were almost totally dependent on the teachings they received verbally from the missionaries.

The demands made on the missionaries were compounded by the fact that the more faithful and prosperous Hawaiian Saints were gathering at the recently established colony on Lanai. Through the sale of produce in Honolulu and other port cities, the colony hoped to finance the entire mission. But until the community became self-sufficient, the enterprise proved to be a severe drain on the resources of members, which, in turn, increased the hardships endured by the missionaries. One Sunday, Joseph F. wrote in his journal, "I tended no meetings as I had no clothes to ware or coat to put on. Brother Simpson begged 25¢ towards getting me a coat. Heard times. Nearly got the bleues, not quite tho. The saints are poor but I am poorer."

Almost as trying as the lack of means was the loss of native leaders to the colony. The branches were populated by Saints who had but a minimal understanding of the Restoration. Consequently, Joseph F. was required to spend most of his time traveling to the various branches, teaching, encouraging, admonishing, and not infrequently excommunicating unworthy members. One memorable occasion illustrates Joseph F.'s understanding of repentance and forgiveness. As recorded in the journal of his companion,

9

Joseph F. stopped at the branch in Nahuna, Maui, where they found that an Elder M., "having fell into sin, repented and asked the saints to forgive him. Brother Joseph called a vote, all voted to forgive him except one self-righteous old man who would not listen to reason nor could show any for not forgiving him, but informed us that he would leave the church if we did not cut M. off. So to save him of the trouble of leaving, we cut him off."

Joseph F.'s leadership abilities, his devotion to missionary work, and his knowledge of the Hawaiian language were quickly noticed by the presiding authorities. After just six months in the field, he was called to preside over three districts on Maui, and three months later, over the entire island. At the age of sixteen, assisted by two other Utah missionaries, Joseph F. had charge of over twelve hundred Saints in two dozen branches. Eight months later, he was sent to preside over the Hilo conferences, and later the Kohala conferences on Hawaii. A year later, he was appointed to preside over the island of Molokai, where he spent the final five months of his mission.

Joseph F. spent more than three years on the islands during his first mission, three years of proselyting without purse or scrip, of scripture study and earnest prayer, of learning about himself and God. It was perhaps the most formative period of his religious life, for at the conclusion of this mission, Joseph F. emerged with a testimony of the gospel and the Restoration that he would never doubt, a testimony that gave purpose and meaning to the rest of his life.

Shortly before his release, he wrote a lengthy letter to one of his favorite cousins, Josephine Coolbrith Smith. "Ina" and her mother had left the Church and moved to Los Angeles. Joseph F. bore his testimony:

I do not wish to "*preach*" to you. . . . I wish you to hear to the counsels of your Fathers, and to the word of God thro' them, but when you revile the principals of Mormonism, you place Barriers immense between your own Dear Self and ethereal fruithon! you shut out the Blessings of God from your heart! hear it and *beware!* do you not know that Mormonism is the foundation upon which I have built? The Life of my soul, the sweetest morsal of my existance, the highth of my pride and ambition? *it is! Tuch* it, and you tuch the apple of my eye, the fiber of my existance! because i *know,*—hear it ye worlds!—I KNOW IT IS TRUE! . . . Mormonism I love. Not with that "Boyish love" that lasts for a time, and changes with each new phase, but with the devotion of Man-hood! The deep, true, earnest love of reason and conviction! . . . I do not care for the world, nor its honors, no more than I do for the bubbles that burst upon the bosome of the wave. . . . My testimony of the Truth is great and powerful. I never can deny it. When I turn traitor to my Lord or perfidious to my Trust, may I that moment seas, and sink into oblivion, that I disgrase no further the object of my Being! let me expire in and for the Cause, for which my Fathers died. I love their hallowed names, and cherish in honor the remembrence of their Noble Spirits. let me, when I meet them again look into their honored faces with complacency, and assurance of an unsullied conscience, and recieve that Boon, that thrice welcomed plaudit, Thou hast fought well the Battle of thy Fathers. Thou hast not been ashamed of thy Savior, neither hast thou shrunk in adversity! A radiant smile from the Parants who gave me Birth, will thrice repay me for an hundread deaths!

Events soon provided opportunities for Joseph F. to demonstrate he was literally willing to lay down his life for the Church. On July 24, 1857, word reached Utah that the president of the United States had dispatched two thousand troops to put down a Mormon "uprising" in Utah. Determined to protect his people by force, if necessary,

Brigham Young ordered the missionaries home. Borrowing thirty dollars from his cousin Silas, Joseph F. obtained passage in the hold of the *Yankee* among the cattle, sheep, and poultry. Arriving in late October, the returning missionaries were met in San Francisco by George Q. Cannon, president of the California mission. President Cannon provided overcoats and blankets for the poorly clad elders, who traveled to San Bernardino in search of employment to pay their way to Zion. Joseph F. was engaged as a teamster, driving a wagon across the desert to Salt Lake City.

One day, after the company had camped for the night, a group of drunken men approached, cursing and threatening to kill any Mormons they saw. According to Joseph Fielding Smith, Jr., several of the Saints hid in the brush, but Joseph F. would not be cowed. Returning with the firewood he had been gathering, he was confronted by the pistol-waving leader of the band, who demanded angrily, "Are you a Mormon?"

Without hesitation, Joseph F. answered boldly, "Yes, siree; dyed in the wool; true blue, through and through." Taken back by the youth's bravado, the man shook his hand in bewilderment and said, "Well, you are the _____ _____ pleasantest man I ever met! Shake, young fellow, I am glad to see a man that stands up for his convictions."

The Utah War and Marriage
(1858-60)

The rest of the trip was made without incident, and upon arriving in Salt Lake City, Joseph F. immediately reported to Brigham Young. He was ready for duty in "the Utah war," and was ordered to be ready for service in Echo Canyon should the federal troops attempt to force their way into the valley. Fortunately, the Church and government soon reached an agreement. Brigham Young would be replaced as territorial governor, on President Buchanan's orders, by Alfred Cummings, and the troops would be allowed to pass through, though not stop in, Salt Lake City.

Partly to dramatize the injustice of sending troops against a peaceful and law-abiding people, Brigham Young ordered the thirty thousand inhabitants of northern Utah to leave their homes and move to southern Utah until it was clear the government would honor their pledges. The evacuation began two weeks after Joseph F.'s return home and continued for two months. When the troops passed through Salt Lake City, they found a deserted city, except for a handful of young men prepared to burn it to the ground if the troops tried to occupy it. Joseph F. and a thousand others were standing by to protect the Saints from any depredations.

In June a full pardon was granted the Mormon "rebels," and the people returned to their homes. Joseph F., who had been ordained a seventy in the meantime, continued to serve in the Utah Militia. In December, he was appointed sergeant-at-arms of the Utah Legislature.

On April 5, 1859, Joseph F. married Levira Smith, daughter of his deceased uncle Samuel H. Smith. He was twenty, she not quite seventeen. Joseph F. and his brother John farmed the family homestead southwest of the city. In October 1859, he was ordained a high priest and served on the Salt Lake Stake high council until called on a mission to England at the April conference, 1860.

First Mission to England
(1860-63)

On April 27, Joseph F. and Levira's brother Samuel H. B. Smith started for England. At Fort Bridger, they waited for Edwin Woolley's wagon train, which had been organized to demonstrate the feasibility of establishing a regular business traffic between Utah and the East. Joseph F. and Samuel H. B. drove Edwin Woolley's mule teams across the plains. On May 10, Apostles Amasa M. Lyman and Charles C. Rich, who were to take charge of the British mission, caught up with the wagon train. At Florence, Nebraska (Winter Quarters), Joseph F. met his brother John, who had come east in the fall to bring their sister, Lovina Smith Walker, and her family to Utah. It had been fourteen years since Joseph F. had seen his older sister.

Arriving at St. Louis on June 20, Joseph F. and Samuel H. B. traveled north to Nauvoo, where Joseph F. said, "I could pick out nearly every spot that I had known in childhood." They stopped in front of Hyrum Smith's old home "and looked at the Office, the Barn, and the little Brick Out house where I shut myself up to keep from going to prison as I supposed." At the Prophet Joseph's home they found Joseph Smith III, who "shook us warmly by the hand and I think felt unfeigned pleasure at seeing us. . . . After chatting a few minutes we went over to the mansion, where we found Frederick and Allicksander who greated us cordially as did Joseph. . . . After dinner Frederick took us in to his mother [Emma Smith Bidamon]. She appeared to have forgotten Samuel but *me* she said she would have known anywhere because I *looked so much like father*!!" Later, Frederick and Alexander took their Utah cousins to the temple ruins, the old Masonic hall, and the homes of Heber C. Kimball and Brigham Young.

One day, after talking over their childhood years, the discussion turned to religion. Joseph III was about to accept a position as head of the church that was to become the Reorganized Church of Jesus Christ of Latter Day Saints. Joseph F. and Samuel H. B. bore their testimonies to him of the truthfulness of the church now headed by Brigham Young before resuming their journey.

On July 14, 1860, Joseph F. and Samuel H. B. Smith set sail from New York with Presidents Lyman and Rich and nine other missionaries bound for Great Britain. They landed at Liverpool thirteen days later. Joseph F. attired himself appropriately as a minister of the gospel in England. "You had ought to see me now," he wrote Levira:

I think you would hardly know whether it was Joseph or not. Let me describe him as he sits. Here he is, hair 'shinggaled,' tall 'stovepipe' hat, stiff collar, and in full English Style, all set and in full trim to go forth a regular English Mormon preacher! and in fact I must confess that I think myself with the rest of the boys appear very respectable, fair examples of the hail, hearty, rugged mountain boys of deseret. . . . We stand quite a show even if they did take us to be wilde beasts and monkeys when we first came.

For three months, Joseph F. had traveled with a dozen other missionaries, often in rather crowded, but economical, conditions. He wrote Levira of his need for time to meditate:

> I think when I get away from so much company my mind will have more time for reflection, both upon the dear ones at home and the calling unto which I am called. I hope I shall ever be able to bear in minde the high trust conferred to me, and realize the importance and magnitude of the position which I holde. May God grant, my dear companion, that I may prove myself worthy of his continued love, and approbation and your affection, and the confidence of my Relatives and friends and the blessings of the servants of God.

Much to their pleasure, Joseph F. and his cousin were assigned to the Sheffield district, where Samuel H.B. had labored during his first mission to England. Samuel was able to familiarize Joseph F. with the area and proselyting methods in England, which were quite different than those of Hawaii. For the first time, Joseph F. was exposed to the challenges and rewards of door-to-door tracting and street meetings. As he later told his missionary sons, he never found it easy to begin tracting or initiate a street meeting, but once into it, he quickly warmed up.

As in Hawaii, the missionaries traveled without purse or scrip, depending upon the hospitality of the local Saints for their support. For the most part, the British Saints were rather poor. They were encouraged to pay tithing and save whatever they could to emigrate to Zion.

Many British branches did not own buildings, but met in homes or in the open air. Notices of open air meetings were usually posted, inviting nonmembers to attend. On one such occasion, Joseph F. encountered stiff, vocal opposition. It was an experience that would enable him to give sound advice to his sons who would have to handle similar situations on their missions:

> As soon as we had done singing a crowd of ruffi-ans set up a most shameful and heartless succession of assaults, by yelling like demons, throwing sods, pushing each other among us, throwing their caps among us, accosting us with every species of abusive language and exhausting every scheme to provoke us to anger, and disturb our peace. During this time I was addressing the people and dodging the sods, the best I could. I was once pushed off my stand, but got up again without ever noticing what passed. I began to appeal to the lovers of peace. Told them we had come to do good, but that if so be, we were allowed to speak. They were judging us before they had heard us, they did not know what we had to tell them. Scripture said 'Prove all things and hold fast to that which was good.' We had not come to force our doctrines upon any. We had come of our own free will. They had done likewise. If they did not want to hear us, leave peacefully. If they stopped, listened attentively, and if we did not tell them the

truth, reject what we said. If we told the truth, they were in duty bound to receive it. At all events we were entitled to respect and protection until we were prove to be imposters, which could never be done, though we were the vilest, if we were not heard. Shame on Englishmen, that would not allow and protect all men in their rights. This was not a heathen land, but a civilized, and enlightened, a religious, a Christian country. We would not disgrace our name and nation, and our enlightenment, by demoralizing, degrading bigotry and religious intolerance. That would be condemned in the dark ages, or in a heathen land! At this, all was quiet. I added a few remarks upon the principles of the gospel and called upon brother Henry Fowler, whom I never heard speak better, or with more power. All listened attentively. At the close of his remarks we closed by singing and prayer, when all hell seemed to be let loose again.

But Joseph F. was not easily discouraged: "We gave out that we would meet again in the afternoon."

On New Year's Eve, after just five months in England, Joseph F. was appointed president of the "Sheffield Pastorate," consisting of the Sheffield, Bradford, Hull, and Lincolnshire conferences. Eleven months later, he reported that the missionaries in his district had baptized 120 new members, and 88 Saints had emigrated to Zion, leaving approximately 900 under his care.

Joseph F. Smith was an indefatigable worker, thoroughly devoted to his duties. But he occasionally found time for relaxation and study. During 1861, as the Civil War raged in the United States, he saw Charles Keen play Hamlet at the Royal Theatre. A few months later, he saw Barry Sullivan play the same role, noting in his journal that though Sullivan gave an excellent performance, he liked Keen better.

17

In addition to scripture study, Joseph F. enjoyed increasing his vocabulary. In his Hawaiian journals he usually reserved a few pages for new words and their definitions—words like *opilation, optimacy, miscreant,* and *econium.* In England, the self-education continued. At one point, he wrote a silly letter to a friend, using all the new words he could:

> Humbly, deprecatingly, and appologetically imploring your Extreeam leniency, and benevolent paliation of my unpardonable inadvertancy in procrastinating to such an incuragible extention, my feeble essay to expaciate in acknowledgement of your eloquential [etc.]

Though not perfect, his spelling had improved over the first Hawaiian letters and diary entries. Significantly, though Joseph F. acquired a large working vocabulary, he rarely used it to impress anyone. He much preferred, as he suggested to his sons, to use expressions easily understood by the reader.

Of all the experiences of Joseph F.'s first mission to England, perhaps the most far-reaching was his association with George Q. Cannon. Ordained an Apostle in August 1860, Elder Cannon was sent to assist President Lyman by publishing the *Millennial Star* and managing the mission's finances. When Presidents Lyman and Rich were released in 1862, Elder Cannon was appointed president. In September, he invited Joseph F. to accompany him and his wife on a tour of the missions in Germany and Denmark. In 1863, Joseph F. was assigned to tour Scotland, meeting with the missionaries and conducting conferences. He was put in charge of the emigration of four thousand Saints who left Europe for Zion that year, a responsibility that required much correspondence with local Church leaders, government officials, and steamship lines. Working closely together, a strong bond grew between Joseph F. Smith and George Q. Cannon that would endure nearly forty years.

As his mission neared an end, Joseph F. wrote, "Prest. Cannon has been most kind and fatherly to me, and if ever a brother sought the welfare of another, Bro. Cannon has sought mine. I owe him boundless grattitude, for the unstinted measure of kindness and Fatherly care he has ever shown me."

One of the most trying aspects of Joseph's three-and-a-half-year mission to England was the chronic bad health of his wife Levira. She eagerly awaited news of his release. In March 1862, he wrote hopefully, "Perhaps you will be surprised to learn that I expect to arrive in Great Salt Lake City in about six weeks!" But he was needed to assist in emigration and was asked to stay until fall, then until April, May, and finally June, 1863. The disappointments of each delay were heartrending to Levira, who had been taking in washing and making rag carpets to support herself and her widowed mother.

Finally, on June 24, 1863, Joseph F. and the Cannons set sail for the United States. Stopping to visit relatives in Illinois, Joseph reached Salt Lake City in late August. He arrived with a four-year-old orphan boy he had adopted in England. Levira was desperately ill. For six weeks Joseph F. sat up every night with his wife, until George A. Smith fairly ordered him to get some sleep.

Second Mission to Hawaii (1864)

Through the winter, Joseph F. nursed his sick wife, but her poor health and nervous condition persisted. In late January, Brigham Young called a special company of missionaries to correct irregularities in the Hawaiian Mission. The company was headed by Apostles Ezra T. Benson and Lorenzo Snow, with former Hawaiian missionaries W. W. Cluff, Alma L. Smith, and Joseph F. Smith.

They left Salt Lake City on March 2, 1864, traveling by stage to Sacramento, then by steamer to San Francisco. Sailing on the twelfth, the company reached Honolulu on March 27, where the Saints "were surprised and rejoiced to see us." Two days later, they took a small schooner to Lahaina, the seaport on Maui where Joseph F. had spent the first month of his mission. Not liking the appearance of the ocean currents, Joseph F. refused to join the others and remained on board to watch their belongings, while natives rowed the missionaries to land. Before the landing party reached shore, the boat capsized. The captain, refusing to drop the forty pieces of silver in his hands, drowned. A boat was sent from shore to rescue the rest, but Elder Snow could not be found. Several minutes later, a native was seen swimming toward the boat with the body. Elder Snow was thought dead, but after reaching land, he was revived.

At Lahaina, the missionaries found the Saints dissatisfied with the condition of the mission and the conduct of its presumed leader, Captain Walter Murray Gibson. Gibson was an adventurer who had joined the Church and convinced Brigham Young to send him on a mission to the Pacific in 1860. The Utah missionaries having been withdrawn during the "Utah War" of 1857-58, Gibson found Hawaii ripe for a takeover. Flaunting his missionary certificate, Gibson had the field to himself. He mixed Church teachings with popular native traditions to win over the people, and set himself up as supreme authority of the mission at the Church colony on Lanai.

On Saturday, the missionaries sailed to Lanai, where they were met by Captain Gibson and his daughter. "Captain Gibson looked warm and thoughtful," Joseph F. recorded, "and received us with a cool and measured formality, at the same time bidding us welcome." On Sunday, they attended Gibson's church services, which were laden with pomp and ceremony. Hoping to avoid an open confrontation, the missionaries held their peace and discussed the situation privately with Gibson on Monday and Tuesday. All Church property and flocks, including 3,700 sheep, 700 goats, and 20 or 30 horses, were in Gibson's name. The natives went to work when Gibson rang the bell and quit when he sounded it again. And he would not yield to priesthood authority.

On Wednesday, April 4, the Apostles called a conference at which the General Authorities of the Church were sustained. In the evening, Elder Benson told the Saints that Gibson had no authority to ordain Apostles, bishops, and "priestesses of the temple" as he had done; that he would not accept counsel and would be cut off. Gibson made an impassioned plea to the people, who, said Joseph F., "were carried completely away, and almost everyone present rose up in an instant, in the midst of considerable excitement. At his order they sat down, and were dismissed."

On Thursday, the missionaries returned to Lahaina on Maui, where a number of Saints, including several who had previously stood with Gibson, expressed their support. Gibson was excommunicated, and his influence was broken. On April 10, the missionaries traveled to Honolulu, where Elder Benson and Snow arranged for passage home. Joseph F. remained, as presiding authority, with William Cluff and Alma L. Smith. They rallied the spirits of the members, baptized new converts, and selected the site for a new Church plantation at Laie. In October, Joseph F. was released.

At Home
(1865-74)

While Joseph F. was in Hawaii, Levira had gone to stay with relatives in San Francisco. When Joseph F. arrived, she refused to return to Salt Lake City, insisting she needed the attention of her California doctor. So Joseph returned to Utah alone, Levira following in July 1865.

Back in Salt Lake City, Joseph F. began his long career in the Church Historian's Office under the supervision of President George A. Smith. He assisted in keeping historical records and occasionally took minutes at meetings of the First Presidency and Council of the Twelve.

In 1865, he was elected to the territorial legislature and served in each succeeding session through 1874. In 1866, he became the recorder and an endowment worker in the Endowment House at three dollars a day. In May, he married Julina Lambson, who had been living in the home of her uncle George A. Smith. Though she had given her consent, Levira was unable to accept polygamy and left her husband, eventually obtaining a divorce in California.

On Sunday afternoon, July 1, 1866, following the regular prayer circle meeting of the First Presidency and the Twelve, President Brigham Young suddenly stopped and said, "Hold on. Shall I do as I feel led? I always feel well to do as the spirit constrains me. It is in my mind to ordain brother Joseph F. Smith to the apostleship and to be one of my councilors." Those present expressing unanimous approval, Joseph F. was ordained, though no public announcement was made until October conference, at which time he was sustained as a member of the Quorum of the Twelve.

In 1868, Joseph married Sarah Ellen Richards, daughter of Willard Richards, and in 1871, Julina's sister, Edna. All three wives and their five children lived together in a house just a few blocks from Temple Square and the Historian's Office.

Second Mission to England
(1874-75)

At the October 1873 conference, Joseph F. was called to preside over the European Mission, which included Great Britain, Scandinavia, Germany, Switzerland, and Holland. He left for his Liverpool headquarters on February 28, 1874, one week after concluding his responsibilities as a member of the territorial legislature. Traveling by train, he reached Washington, D.C., on March 7, where he visited Utah's delegate to Congress, George Q. Cannon. Elder Cannon introduced him to President Ulysses S.

Grant, and gave his fellow Apostle a tour of the nation's capital. On March 10, Joseph F. sailed from New York, arriving in Liverpool on the twenty-first.

In England, Joseph F. enjoyed the association of several men who later played prominent roles in the history of the Church: L. John Nuttall, secretary to the First Presidency; Joseph's cousin John Henry Smith, later an Apostle and Counselor in the First Presidency; and Francis M. Lyman, another cousin who became an Apostle and served as President of the Quorum of the Twelve for thirteen years.

During 1874, 513 converts were baptized in England, 94 in the Swiss-German mission, and 935 in Scandinavia. Two thousand Saints emigrated to Utah. But the following year the number of emigrants was cut in half. The Perpetual Emigration Fund had run out of money, and the Saints relied on Joseph F. to help raise funds locally for them to gather in Zion.

Through the summer of 1875, George A. Smith's health was failing. John Henry was released to attend to his father, and on September 2, Joseph F. received a cable notifying him that President George A. Smith had passed away. Joseph F. wrote in his journal:

> I cannot tell with what terrible weight this melancholy intelligence fell upon my soul. On no other man in the church did greater responsibility rest. . . . The world has lost a bright light and an honest man, the saints a wise and faithful counsellor, a prophet, seer and revelator, and as true a friend of Christ the Lord. As for myself, I feel as though he were my own father, and my greatest earthly benefactor.

A few days later came word of Joseph F.'s release. He arrived in the Ogden railroad station October 1. On hand to greet him were Orson Pratt, George Q. Cannon, Samuel

H. B. Smith, "Aunt Bathsheba" (George A.'s widow), John Henry Smith, Brigham Young, Jr., and others who had come in a special train car to meet him. Arriving in Salt Lake City, Joseph F. reported immediately to Brigham Young and then went home to his family, whom he found "expectantly awaiting my arrival. All as poor and thin as weasles, but in good health, and spent most of the night visiting and examining contents of my trunk and valise in gratification of the universal female characteristic curiosity, after which we retired to rest."

**At Home
(1875-77)**

In keeping with Brigham Young's policy of appointing Apostles to preside over geographic areas of the Church, Joseph F. was given jurisdiction over Davis county, north of Salt Lake county. In addition to his ecclesiastical responsibilities, Joseph F. was made president of the Davis County Cooperative Company, which consisted of several small co-ops, including a tannery and shoe shop. He consolidated the various small enterprises, with the bishops of Layton, Kaysville, Farmington, Centerville, and Bountiful as the board of directors. Stock was sold to raise capital and make improvements in the tannery and boot shop; open a butchering operation; augment the cooperative's cattle, horse, and sheep herds; and fund other projects. In addition to these duties, Joseph F. continued to work in the Endowment House and at the Historian's Office.

**Final Mission to England
(1877)**

At the April 1877 conference, Joseph F. was called to return to England to preside once again over the European Mission. This time he was permitted to take his wife Sarah and four-year-old son Joseph Richards with him. He was accompanied by Charles W. Nibley, who soon became Joseph F.'s closest friend and later Presiding Bishop of the Church.

Arriving in Liverpool in May 1877, Joseph F. found the British Mission in poor condition. Little, if any, outdoor preaching had been done since he had left in 1875, and financially "the mission is flat as a pancake, broke entirely." There was no money from the Perpetual Emigration Fund to help the Saints emigrate, and tithing had dropped to half of what it had been in 1875. He wrote:

> Our meeting rooms are small and generally in unfavorable localities (where we have any) owing to the poverty of the people. But few will go into them, except to interrupt, ridicule or take notes for scandle. But many will listen to us in the streets and squares and byways, though this course subjects us to much clamour and insult, sometimes abuse, generally lead on by religious bigots. . . . Scarcely an individual joins the church but some 'parson,' or scripture-reader follows right up on the track, with his slanders and misrepresentations with a view to disuade the candidate or convert from what they style the perdition of Mormonism.

Traveling throughout the mission, Joseph F. soon contracted the cold that plagued him through all his previous years there, and was intermittently afflicted with lumbago and eyestrain. Nevertheless, he maintained a steady and demanding pace to inspire effective proselyting among the missionaries and faithful among the members.

In August, Orson Pratt arrived to consult with British phoneticists and shorthand experts. Brigham Young had directed Elder Pratt to devise a new phonetic system of spelling and publish the standard works, along with appropriate primers and grammars, in England. Lorus Pratt acted as secretary to his father, who was also dividing the Book of Mormon into verses and adding marginal references.

Near the end of the month, Joseph F. had the recurring premonition that "some great event was about to happen." He thought that perhaps Queen Victoria was about to die. Then, on August 22, Orson Pratt related a dream he had had about Brigham Young the night before:

> He saw him riding in his carriage, when suddenly his horses took a fright and dashed down a steep bank into a deep river or stream of water, rushed through the stream and up the abrupt and seemingly impossible declivity on the other side. We all decided, if the dream indicated anything, it meant some sudden difficulty or trouble through which the president would have to pass.

Eight days later, the news of the death of President Young arrived, and Joseph F. was called home to assist in the transition to a new Church administration.

Joseph F. Smith as Missionary

By the time his sons started on their missions, Joseph F. Smith had acquired nine years of invaluable missionary experience. He had traveled to his assignments on horseback, mule team, stage, sailing ships, and steamers. He had lived among the poorest of God's children in Hawaii, sharing their deprivations and rejoicing in their simple but powerful faith. He had overcome a lack of formal education to become a scriptorian and a powerful speaker. Even as a teenager his strong testimony and dedication to hard work were recognized as qualities that would place him as a leader of men many years his senior. In England, he quieted determined hecklers with commanding dignity and appeal to reason. As mission president, he gained vast experience with the diverse problems encountered by missionaries, and their solutions.

Perhaps as important as his missionary experiences was Joseph F.'s intimate acquaintance with the events and people at the roots of the Restoration. He himself had lived in Nauvoo and remembered the martyrdom, Winter Quarters, and the trek to Utah. Brigham Young, George A. Smith, Heber C. Kimball, Orson Pratt, and other leading authorities were his advisors and associates. They recognized in Joseph F. Smith a man of boundless energy and devotion to Zion. As a result, at sixteen, he was a missionary; at twenty, a member of the Salt Lake Stake high council; at twenty-seven, an Apostle; and at thirty-five, presiding authority over all missions in Europe, Africa, and Australia.

Many aspects of missionary work have changed over the past hundred years. Missionaries no longer travel without purse or scrip. They are no longer charged with the responsibility of regulating Church activities in their areas. Yet the essential elements of proclaiming the gospel of Jesus Christ remain unchanged, the qualifications for the ministry are constant, and the opportunities for service and personal growth are as great. The advice Joseph F. Smith offered his missionary sons is as valuable for modern missionaries as it was for them.

—Scott G. Kenney

Hyrum M.
(1895-98)

The death of Brigham Young brought Joseph F.'s final proselyting mission to an unexpected end. In the intervening years before his first son was called on a mission, much transpired. In 1880, the First Presidency was organized with John Taylor as President and George Q. Cannon and Joseph F. Smith as his counselors. Francis M. Lyman and John Henry Smith were called into the Quorum of the Twelve at the same time.

In 1882, Joseph F.'s colleague from his first Hawaiian mission, John T. Caine, was elected Utah's delegate to Congress, and Joseph F. presided over Utah's 1882 constitutional convention. Instead of admitting Utah to the Union, however, Congress passed legislation making plural marriage a crime and placing the government of Utah in the hands of a five-man committee appointed by the president of the United States.

The following year, on December 6, 1883, Joseph F. married Heber C. Kimball's daughter, Alice Ann, and adopted her three children by a previous marriage. And six weeks later he married John Taylor's niece, Mary Taylor Schwartz.

From September 1884 to September 1891, Joseph F. was "on the underground," avoiding federal marshals who hoped not only to prosecute him for polygamy, but to extract information from him regarding other plural families he knew from his service as recorder in the Endowment House. Visits to his families were infrequent due to the surveillance of the marshals and their spies. But he was able to take Julina with him to Hawaii for most of his exile from January 1885 to July 1887. He returned to Utah just in time to be at President John Taylor's side when he died.

In February 1888, Joseph F. was sent to Washington, D.C., where he was not likely to be recognized, to coordinate Utah's efforts to gain statehood. In the spring of 1889, he returned to be present at the reorganization of the First Presidency: Wilford Woodruff, President, and George Q. Cannon and Joseph F. Smith, Counselors. President Woodruff issued the Manifesto, declaring an end to plural marriage on September 25, 1890, but it was not until September 7, 1891, that Joseph F. was finally granted a presidential amnesty, which freed him from a life of seclusion and secrecy.

The Manifesto relieved the Church of a great deal of pressure, but the property escheated by the government would not be returned for several years. The years of "the raid" had been costly, and when the panic of 1893 hit Utah, the Church was pushed to the edge of bankruptcy. Small investors, like Joseph F., were nearly wiped out. Since 1884, he had tried to maintain separate households for each of his five wives, and by the time Hyrum M. left on his mission, Joseph F. was supporting thirty-four children. Four more were born during Hyrum's absence. Financially, Joseph F. and the Church were struggling. Joseph F. had to borrow $500 to pay his taxes in 1895, and was forced to sell property in Idaho at a loss to pay his taxes the next year. Still, he managed to send Hyrum M. $10 or $15 every month, and traveled to New York to meet his returning son in February 1898.

Hyrum M., the eldest son of Joseph F. and Edna Lambson Smith, was born March 21, 1872. Hyrum M. married Ida Bowman on November 15, 1895, the day before leaving on his mission. Three weeks later, he was in England, assigned to Leeds, where he was soon given responsibility for the Leeds, Bradford, Hull, Sheffield, and Lincolnshire conferences. A year later, he was transferred to Westoe, just south of the Scottish border. His mission president was Anthon H. Lund, later Joseph F.'s counselor in the First Presidency.

Overcoming Fear of Speaking

Hyrum's first letter from England arrived December 17, 1895. The scenes he described recalled many memories for Joseph F. of his first mission to England. Joseph F. wrote Hyrum of the difficulty he experienced speaking in street meetings and offered good advice to missionaries who experience fear in public speaking.

December 17, 1895

It was in Hunslet-Lane near Leeds where I made my maiden outdoor speech, and arrested the attention of pedestrians after Samuel [first cousin Samuel H. B. Smith] and a native Elder named Woodhead had failed to do it. And when I got through, an old man cried out: "Well! There is nothink bad about that, but my advise (h)is you'd better not 'ave anythink to do with (h)any ov-um!!" And they all seemed to take his advice. At that time nothing I had attempted was so hard for me to do as to try to speak out in the open air, but when I "broke the ice," I was as happy as a bird. It gave me strength, for the Spirit of the Lord helped me. And, so it will you and your companions if you courageously meet obstacles, with a firm determination to do your whole duty. Get in your hearts the Spirit of God, the knowledge of the truth, and determination to do right, and you need not fear the taunts nor ridicule, nor the wisdom or learning of any man. Keep away from toughs and from their haunts and pay attention to study and prayer, always remembering God in humility.

The Importance of Letter Writing

It was the middle of January, and the family had not heard from Hyrum for nearly three weeks. From his own missionary experience, Joseph F. understood the importance of letters from home and wrote to his son regularly, always answering Hyrum's letters immediately and in his own hand. Hyrum had yet to develop these qualities to his father's satisfaction. But rather than chastise, Joseph F. patiently pointed out the problems that might contribute to his neglect, and encouraged his son to a greater awareness of his responsibility.

January 15, 1896

I suppose you have been busy, that your time has been occupied with other duties, and you have not written as often as we would like. There is something of an art in letter writing, which can be acquired only by practice. It is very desirable for you to improve as much as you can in the art of corresponding. You must not allow yourself to be supine. Energy is the vitalizing force which leads on to success and triumph. It is energy which has developed greatness in men, more than natural talent. Many a man with meager ability has made his mark in the world through being energetic and persistent, while many and many a man with superior native talent has completely failed for the sole want of energy. Whatever is worth doing is worth doing well. Whatever you engage in, concentrate your mind and effort upon it and do it as thoroughly as you can. Time is precious, let not a moment be wasted in vain regrets, in discouragement, or fear to try or to *begin* to do. You have not had to rustle at home to make ends meet, nor to *save* time and utilize it. You may now find it necessary, therefore, to redouble your *vigor* and *energy* to meet the demands of duty. One of those demands . . . is to write good, kind letters to your wife.

Clothes and Character

Hyrum had been in England two months when he sent home a photograph of himself and his companions, all well dressed and wearing top hats, the mark of an English gentleman at the time. Although pleased with his son's striking appearance, Joseph F. reminded Hyrum that fashion is no substitute for character.

February 27, 1896

Two days ago Mamma received two photos of a group of nine Elders including yourself and brother Davis. Mamma was highly elated, and all of us were exceedingly pleased with the picture. Someone remarked it was a "good display of silk hats." For my own part I was pleased to see you each had a "dress" hat, and that you all presented so good an appearance. There is very much, after all, in presentable rainment in the eyes of the world. . . . But the *real* thing—the *substance* must lie within. And good clothing, however costly or genteel, can never supply the lack of understanding, good breeding, and a knowledge of true principle. Of this you are fully aware. A man of intelligence will, even in ordinary clothing, always out-strip the fool in soft rainment. While I would always be pleased to see my boys well clad, in goodly rainment, I would much rather see them display meekly and wisely, minds well stored with useful information, and well seasoned with common sense, always tempered with pure and honorable charity and God-like love. . . . My hope in you is built upon your unswerving integrity to the truth, and your unyielding honor before God and man. Remember the old saw:
Honors kings can give,
Honor they can't
Honors without honor
Is a barren grant!

A Mother's Love

On March 16, word reached Joseph F. that his son Joseph Richards Smith (Buddie) had suffered an acute attack of appendicitis and would have to be operated on immediately to save his life. He wrote:

> I hastened home—it was raining, cloudy and dark. I found him lying on blankets and pillows on the floor, in great distress, although under the influence of an opiate. I felt I would give all I had for his life, and I said, "Go ahead!" But before preparation for the "butchery"—as it seemed to all of us—was completed, it was 5 p.m.—still raining and dismal—and as to the necessary light, very unpropitious for so painful and dangerous an operation. However, by the aid of lamps the operation was performed within an hour and three-quarters time, and Buddie was laid on the bed.

Fearful for Buddie's precarious hold on life, Joseph F. and his wife Sarah Ellen Richards remained by his bedside. In his next letter to Hyrum, Joseph F. revealed his sensitivity to the unique love a mother feels for her children, giving support to the great commandment, "Honour thy father and thy mother." (Ex. 20:12.)

March 23, 1896

His mother and I have stuck to him night and day (his mamma both night and day, and I, of night only) since the operation. . . . His mother has thought *only* of him and faithfully ministered to his needs, and the feeling and sense most stirred in my mind by the example of a devotion which only springs from a *mother's love*, such as Buddie's mother has shown him, can only be requited, it seems to me, by the truest and most tender regard on the part of children for their mother. The purest and most unselfish love on earth is mother's love! It is typical of and next the pure love of God! The child who would so far forget himself and his highest duty to mortal beings, as to permit him or herself to do an act that would grieve the heart of a mother (without great cause) deserves the keenest punishment. I feel that my children, one and all, are firmly bound by nature's highest law to love and honor, cherish and revere, to nurture and protect, *her* who bore them into the world.

If my children will never fail to do their whole duty to their mothers, I will guarantee their fidelity to me! For they have known, still know and shall continue in the knowledge of *the fact*, that I have been, am, and will continue to be, to the extent of my ability, true to them— both to mothers and their children. I need not say to you, "Honor thy father and thy mother," for I believe you do.

The Model of Righteousness

Hyrum's mission president was Anthon H. Lund, later a Counselor in the First Presidency to Joseph F. Smith. In his letters home, Hyrum often referred to President Lund with great respect, fondness, and admiration, prompting this response from Joseph F.

March 23, 1896

I am pleased with your references to President Lund, for I regard him as a choice, spirited, intelligent man. Cultivate the confidence and love, and seek the acquaintance of the pure and good; and try to absorb the best and noblest qualities of the best men. No man can aim higher than to seek to possess himself of the characteristics of Jesus of Nazareth. He was and is the grandest type of Man-hood who was ever clothed in flesh and blood on this earth. The man who succeeds in reaching nearest to his attributes and perfection will get nearest to God! Next to the Son, Himself!! I do not mean that anyone should be self-righteous. Self-righteousness is abhorrent and most *UN*like the Son of God. He that *doeth* righteously, and vaunts not of it, is righteous.

Discerning the Truth

Truth will always appeal to the judgment of a man who is humble, honest, clean, and possessed of the Holy Ghost. And such an one will always be able to detect error and sin. The Spirit of God can and will operate upon the mind which is clean and pure. It is the mind diseased and contaminated with sin or the love of sin, or the love of worldly gains or pleasures, by selfishness or other sordid dross, which cannot discern the *truth* from error. For the Spirit of Light and Truth cannot affiliate with, nor operate upon, the mind in such condition.

Economy

The panic of 1893 had cut severely into the Mormon economy. The Church was forced to borrow heavily to meet its obligations and help support the industries that provided jobs for its members. As a member of the First Presidency, Joseph F. Smith felt keenly the financial stringency of the times. In just two years the Church would have to sell a million dollars in short-term bonds to meet its obligations.

The hard times were aggravated by a mining disaster in Ogden Canyon that killed five and injured five more. They were, as Joseph F. noted, "Brethren whose families have been suddenly deprived of the winners of their bread, and protectors and companions."

The Smith family also suffered its share of financial strain, including the $300 appendectomy on son Joseph Richards Smith. Hyrum mentioned the cold and damp

36

weather in England and expressed a need to purchase warmer clothing, to which his father replied.

April 9, 1896

I know you will use your means prudently—I want you to put your trust in the Lord, and only use means as you really need. I know what the English climate is, and I want you to be properly clad. A light overcoat may be a necessity to save you from a cold, and possible sickness. Get a good one and have it to use when needed—the same with pants or stockings, or other clothing.

My policy, as you know, has always been to take *good care* of what the Lord gives me, and so I have never lacked. True, I have never had much, if any, surplus, but always enough for my actual necessities, and some little to give to the poor. I think any man who has provided for a family as large or as numerous as mine has done a good work, and is entitled to some credit for economy, considering the limited resources which have fallen to my lot, at least. But I give God, and my precious companions, all honor and credit for my prosperity and success.

Association with and Work for the Dead

As Hyrum matured in his knowledge of the gospel and continued to preach in England, doctrinal questions occasionally arose in his mind. Who was better qualified than his father to answer them? On April 14, 1896, Hyrum wrote, posing several questions. Two of Joseph F. Smith's responses follow.

May 18, 1896

In reply to your question: "To what extent do our relatives and friends who have died have cognizance of us and our actions?" That will depend on the condition

of our departed kindred and friends. All spirits are subject
to the laws of the spirit world. For instance, the Prophet
Joseph Smith, on October 9, 1843, said: "Spirits can only
be revealed in flaming fire or glory. (That is, disembodied
spirits.) Angels have advanced further, their light and
glory being tabernacled, and hence, they appear in bodily
shape. (Angels here referred to are resurrected beings.)
The spirits of just men are made ministering servants to
those who are sealed unto life eternal, and it is through
them that the sealing power comes down. (As in the case of
the administrations of John the Baptist in the act of
conferring the Aaronic Priesthood, and Peter and James
conferring the Melchizedek Priesthood, John not yet
having tasted death, and also in the case of Moroni, in
restoring the Nephite records, and also as revealed in the
Kirtland Temple, by Moses, Elias, Elijah, D&C Section
110.) But Joseph continues: "The spirits of the just are
exalted to a greater and more glorious work; hence they
are blessed in their departure to the World of Spirits.
Enveloped in flaming fire *they are not far from us* and know
and understand our thoughts and feelings and notions
and are *often pained therewith.*" . . . Now, if our departed
kindred and friends are just (righteous) spirits, exalted
to this greater and more glorious work, they may be very
near us, enveloped in flaming glory, taking notes, or
observing actions of our thought, feelings, and actions,
rejoicing because of our virtues and integrity to the truth,
or sorrowing and weeping over our sins and
transgressions. And not only so, but able to render
assistance, when our spirits are susceptible to the power
they wield. You will find in the Pearl of Great Price
[Moses 7:28] that God and the heavens wept, and the
reasons why. You must bear in mind, my Son, that "all
things whatsoever God of His infinite wisdom has seen
fit and proper to reveal to us while we are dwelling in
mortality, in regard to our mortal bodies, are revealed
to us in the abstract, and independent of affinity of this

38

mortal tabernacle, but are revealed to our spirits precisely as though we had no bodies at all, and those revelations which will save our spirits will save our bodies. God reveals them to us in view of no eternal dissolution of the body, or tabernacle." (*Compendium*, page 284, paragraph 1.) I believe that our departed kindred and loved ones are far more mindful of us and solicitous for our salvation day by day than they ever were in the flesh, because they know more. As you will find in Malachi 4:5-6, "Behold, I will send you Elijah the Prophet," and etc., . . . "and he shall turn the hearts of the fathers to the children," and etc. And in the D&C, Section 128:18, "We are the children. The fathers have gone before." Joseph says: "The greatest responsibility in this world that God has laid upon us is to seek after the dead." The apostle says, "They without us cannot be made perfect, for it is necessary that the sealing power should be in our hands to seal our children and our dead for the fullness of the dispensation of times, and etc." *Compendium*, page 284, under heading "All revelations are Spiritual."

Guardian Angels

In reply to your question: "Do we all have guardian angels, and is the *Key to Theology* authentic on this subject, pages 117 to 119?"

To both of these propositions, I can answer *yes*, so far as I have been taught and am able to learn. Jesus said (Matthew 18:10): "Take heed that ye despise not one of these little ones; for I say unto you that in Heaven their angels do always behold the face of my Father which is in Heaven." This is no exception to the rule. The rule applies to all of God's children or little ones. But, the guardian angels of the pure, the innocent "which believe in me," as Jesus said, verse 6, are they which "do always behold the face of my Father." While those guardian angels of the disobedient, and etc., I would infer, cannot always bring up in remembrance before the Father such as are disobedient, and believe not in Christ.

Teaching with Prudence

In May 1896, Joseph F. Smith received a letter from Hyrum, describing an experience recorded in Hyrum's journal on May 1.

> It has been a nice, fine day and I have remained indoors nearly all day. Wrote a letter home and this evening Brothers Winder, Brough, Schofield and myself went down town and held an open air meeting, and a meeting it was to be sure, and I received an experience that I will never forget. We took our stand under a lamp on Earl Street off Manchester Road, and commenced singing the hymn, page 143, then prayer, then hymn 343. Quite a crowd gathered and Brother Winder talked to them for over half an hour. He then asked me if I cared to speak. Was not very anxious—he considered it my duty to bear my testimony. I had not been speaking long when I was interrupted by an old man. I made the assertion that no person could be saved, but by obedience to the principles of the gospel, one of which was baptism by immersion. The "thief" was sprung. The old gent was soon quieted on that score. Finally he yelled out, "I know who you are, you're a L.D.S." then to the crowd he said, "that man is a L.D.S. He believes in polygamy and has got a half-dozen wives." With this, an old lady who had been championing us and upbraiding all who interfered or interrupted us exclaimed, "What are you, a L.D.S.? Mormons! Great God!" and with a wild gesture made for the outer edge of the crowd.

The devil seemed to enter into the crowd and convert it into a mob, for they closed in upon me, and with shoving and crowding began to jostle me out of the street into Manchester Road. The cry of "hit him," "knock him down," etc. frequently heard. I drew my remarks to a close and after several men and women had been pushed down, managed to get out of the crowd, where I joined my brethren, got my hat and umbrella and together started on a good walk . . . with a large crowd closely following. A small boy or girl occasionally ran up behind us and struck us or threw pebbles at us. As we got out of town, the mob gradually left us, and we got home all right.

This experience stimulated Joseph F.'s memory of a similar experience he had had on his first mission to England in 1860.

May 18, 1896

Your welcome favors of April 14th and April 18th are both before me, and there is another from you at home, the date of which I do not remember, giving an account of your first experience in an English mob. I have seen them perform myself, and I know what it is like. But I never but once was the cause of a disturbance. That was in Sheffield, during my first experience in speaking English. (Previous to that I had been to the Islands.) We had a large audience. William M. Gibson, a great preacher, was present, but I was speaking, and I said that "the authority of the apostles of today was the same as that held by the apostles of Christ's day, and that the word of modern apostles was as good as the word of the ancient apostles!" Somebody in the audience cried out, "Blasphemy!" This was too much for my boyish temper to bear. The proposition I had made seemed so clear, so

41

plain, and so indisputable to my mind, I could not brook
a shout of "Blasphemy," and let loose on my opponent
upon apostate Christianity, hireling ministers and upon
those opposed to the truth in general, in my best licks,
and by the time I got through, I had stirred up the
emissaries of his Satanic Majesty until they were red hot,
and the parrot and monkey show began in good shape!
Brother Gibson tried to quell the riot, but the excited mob
would not listen to him, would not hear any more, and
made for our stand! We slipped through the crowd and
made for home. But some of the leaders were aching to
get hold of *me*, and hung round for hours to get a chance.
Well, this experience taught me a good lesson. Thereafter,
I moderated my fervor, became more diplomatic in the
presence of a mixed crowd, and avoided showing any
temper when reviled. In fact, I learned to be reviled
without reviling back again, to take an insult without
retorting, except in meekness and gentlemanly candor.
Many times after this I succeeded in quelling excitement
and pouring oil upon the troubled waters, but never in
exciting violence. I always tried to make my hearers feel
that I and my associates were peacemakers, and lovers
of peace and good-will, that our mission was to save, and
not destroy, to build up and not tear down; to preach and
show a better way without referring to the poorer ways
until the sympathy of the audience was gained. Still, the
Devil was never, and will never, be reconciled to the truth,
and there are unreasoning creatures, sightless, deaf, and
invulnerable to common sense, who will be content with
nothing but malicious opposition to the cause of Zion.
From such, turn away! Time and breath spent upon such
are time and breath thrown away. They are aptly
described by the apostle Peter in his 2nd Epistle, 2nd
chapter. Read it carefully. There is an old saying and a
true one that honey will catch more flies than vinegar.
Kindness will beget friendship and favor, but anger or
passion will drive away sympathy. To win one's respect

and confidence, approach him mildly, kindly. No friendship was ever gained by an attack upon principle or upon man, but by calm reason and the lowly Spirit of Truth. If you have built for a man a better house than his own, and he is willing to accept yours and forsake his, then, and not till then, should you proceed to tear down the old structure. Rotten though it may be, it will require some time for it to lose *all* its charms and fond memories of its former occupant. Therefore let *him,* not *you,* proceed to tear it away. Kindness and courtesy are the primal elements of gentility. "For politness is to do and say, the kindest things in the kindest way!"

Avoiding Arguments

After a meeting in Bradford, Yorkshire, England, a minister approached Hyrum and asked for a conversation. Hyrum recounted the incident, which developed into quite a contentious discussion. Joseph F. responded with counsel and love, admonishing Hyrum to avoid arguments and describing the proper method of proclaiming the gospel.

May 20, 1896

Your description of the discussion with the minister was particularly impressive to the folks. But, my son, do not waste breath nor time in discussions, arguments, or contentions with any such characters. If anybody asks a question, whether he asks it civilly or not, answer it civilly, but decline to contend. There is a great difference between *reasoning*, and contention. Discussion nearly always runs into contention, and that is not of the Lord, nor at all wise. I can understand you well, and I know how hard it is to decline a banter to discuss questions. I have been in it myself, and your disposition is much like my own. Experience has taught me that where calm statements of fact and mild reasoning will not prevail or succeed, there

43

is no use to enter into discussions and arguments. Say to the people: "We have not come to contend with you. All men are free to choose their own course and believe what they please, but, that we have that *we* believe to be truth, eternal truth, and we simply want to tell the people of it." And then leave them to receive or reject it as they choose. You must take care that your earnestness be not carried to the extent, as mine has often been, to be mistaken for anger. Of course, you will have to learn by experience all these things. But put your trust in the Lord. Be calm, truthful and moderate, and fear not the face of man! Nor shrink from any.

June 3, 1896

God bless you my son. *Keep Cool* before the public. Be calm and passionless in outdoor speaking. Avoid [contention with] all men, that perchance thereby we may bring some few to a knowledge of the truth. A few simple facts, or Gospel Truth, simply but earnestly and calmly told will find their own way into the hearts of the honest, if listened to, while volumes of eloquence will only be wasted upon the comeup and dishonest. God bless my boy.

Confidence and Courtesy

On June 18, 1896, Hyrum described an encounter with a Methodist minister. Again, Joseph F. discussed the incident carefully and with wisdom and love developed a lesson for Hyrum's betterment.

July 31, 1896

In your postscript "from Bradford," you mentioned a conversation you had had with a Methodist preacher, who had studied the Bible for 40 years, and etc. You say "I told him he must have been a dreadfully dull student to have been studying the Bible for 40 years and still to know so little about it."

This statement as you make it is without doubt the naked truth, but, my Son, if you said it in just those words, was it not a little too *naked*? Objectionable facts should always be clothed in as mild and unobjectionable language as possible.

Perhaps you did this in that way and in relating the matter to us told it bluntly. Again, when he began abusing the Latter-Day Saints you say, "I plainly told him that I would not take such abuse from him nor any other man; he apologized and I bid him good afternoon." I am glad he "apologized," for that would indicate that he had at least a modicum of the elements necessary to the character of a gentleman. Had he been an unmitigated "galute," he would not have made any apology, but might have become violent and undertaken to put you out of his house, as I suppose you were in his house, because of your saying, you were "invited into the house of one man who said he was a local preacher of the Methodist persuasion" and etc. Now, what I want to say to you, my Son, is this: I would not like you to cultivate abrupt manners, nor the use of harsh words even to your, or our, worst enemies. You know what Paul says are the fruits of the spirit, and the spirit is what you must cultivate in order to succeed well. For instance: Ephesians 5:9-10, "for the fruit of the spirit is in all goodness and righteousness and truth, proving what is acceptable unto the Lord." And again: Galatians 5:22-25, "But the fruit of the spirit is *love,* joy, *peace, longsuffering, gentleness,* goodness, faith, meekness, temperance: *against such there is no law.* And they that are Christ's have crucified the flesh with the affections and lusts. If we live in the Spirit let us also walk in the Spirit." And etc. James 3:17-18 says: "But the wisdom that is from above is first *pure,* then peaceable, gentle and easy to be intreated, full of mercy and good fruits, without partiality and without hypocrisy. And the fruit of righteousness is sown in peace of them that make peace." Now the fact is, as you have had abundant opportunity to know already, that all opponents of "Mormonism" (so called) possess the spirit of anger, of hatred, strife, contention, bitterness, of false accusation, of wickedness, and of ignorance, and often of murder. All such do the works of the flesh which are these: Galatians 5:19-21, "*adultery, fornication, uncleanness,* lasciviousness, idolatry, witchcraft, *hatred, variance,* emulations, *wrath, strife,* seditions, heresies, envyings, murders, drunkenness, revellings, and such like: . . . They which do such things shall not inherit the Kingdom of God." Such as these we should avoid except where duty calls, or where accident, or by design on their part, we might be brought in contact with them. And *then* we should never, *no never,* descend to their methods, their spirit, nor their character. Always maintain a calm, peaceable demeanor. Keep cool! Let ignorance expend itself in impotent wrath, but let the truth stand still with patient dignity and calmness, to strike its deliberate, effective blow at just the right moment. Then it will knock its opponent out with scarcely an effort. For "Truth is mighty and will prevail." You have the truth. Use it, defend it by the *spirit* of truth. You may not know it all, no man does! Any one who assumes to know it all is a fool whose folly will surely manifest itself as if upon the housetop.

Only God knows all things or comprehends all truth. Therefore do not be discouraged for a moment because there is much for you to learn, or because others may know more than you. Our cause is good, and just, and right, and its aim is pure, noble and great! *You know* this, as well as I—as well as any man *can* know anything. This you can maintain by your own experience, and by the testimony of God's Spirit in your soul, and by history and by the word of God in the Books.

So far, you *know* you are right, and you can afford to keep cool and calm over any contention on these points. He is strong who hath the truth, he is "thrice armed" who battles for the right. And he who strives calmly in God's might, and not in his own strength, will be victorious. But while we should always hope and pray for victory, we must not lose sight of the fact that all others are also seeking victory. We should always aim to *help them* to victory, not to defeat them! Our aim is life eternal, our object to lift up mankind, not debase them. The enemy of the truth always seeks to dishonor and debase the truth and its advocates. The *friend* of the truth who would pursue a similar course descends to the level of the enemy of truth, at least in his efforts, and, so far, is no wiser nor better than he. Therefore, my Son, (2 Timothy 2:6-7), "The husbandman that laboreth must be *first partaker* of the fruits. Consider what I say; and the Lord give thee understanding in all things." Treat all men courteously. Be kind to the erring. "Blessed are the merciful for they shall obtain mercy." If reviled, revile not. If persecuted, put your trust in the Lord. "Love them that hate you." Do to others as you would that they should do to you. For this is the true gospel spirit, it is the law of God, it is the Gospel itself which you are to preach. You must also practice it. What ever other men are, you must be a gentleman and a true man. Nothing can repay you for the loss of manhood and true gentility. A man may be much of a gentleman and know but little, if anything, about the Gospel. But, a man cannot be a true and faithful Latter-Day Saint without being a true gentleman. General Washington took off his hat and bowed to a Negro servant. When remonstrated by a proud officer for such obeisance to a menial, the great Washington replied: "I cannot afford to be less polite than my servant!" We learn to do by doing and doing right makes righteous men. I hope you will receive the foregoing in the good spirit in which it is written.

A Father's Prayer

In a beautiful expression of love and faith, Joseph F. prayed for the well-being and success of his missionary son.

September 4, 1896

Your welcome favor of August 22 came to hand on the 2nd inst. and we were all glad to hear from our absent loved one. We never pray but we remember you and your companions in the missionary field. And our prayer is that God may remember you and all of us better than we remember Him; that He will deal most kindly and lovingly with you, raise up friends in the midst of strangers, soften the hearts of the unbelieving, and open their eyes and unstop their ears that they may see and hear and understand the truth which will make them free; that the merciful Father may shield you and your associates and co-laborers from violence, from malice, from snares and plots, from cold and hunger, from cruel exposures to cruel elements, from all the pleasing wiles of the Tempter, from the sirenizing influence of woman, and from every wrong and from every evil, that the Holy Spirit may dwell in you—inspire you with courage, with hope, with faith, with charity and with pure knowledge, and make you not only valiant for the truth, but wise and prudent. O! God bless my son who is out in Thy vineyard, and all his brothers at home, and his companions and fellow laborers abroad. Make them polished shafts in Thine hand and clothe them with mighty power from on High. Put Thy gracious spirit into their hearts, and stir their souls to the depths with Thy precious love. Make them to utter Thy word in meekness but in the power and demonstration of the Holy Ghost. And keep them always within the sound of the still, small voice of the Spirit which whispers consolation, assurance, peace, and comfort, and warning and admonition to the awakened Soul. O! Bless them and comfort them, and keep them in Thine own good hand; make them to see, and know, and feel that Thou art God with whom there is no variableness nor shadow of turning, and that they are, indeed, Thy sons! And so keep them in Thy paths all the days of their lives, that they may be faithful into death, and unto endless life, and joy and exaltation in Thy glorious Kingdom. . . .

Oh! May God my Father bless you with life, health, strength, wisdom, knowledge, humility and integrity, that you may never falter nor fail. My son, our Father is good, and we will be true to Him though He may try us. May you prosper now and forever, is my earnest prayer.

In the same letter, Joseph F. commented on the gift of the Holy Ghost.

Only those who are "born again" can "see the kingdom of heaven." And not always are those "born of the water" also "born of the Spirit." In other words, not every one who is baptized receives the Holy Ghost, notwithstanding, the "gift" may be bestowed. You know there is a difference between the Holy Ghost, and the *gift* of the Holy Ghost. The Prophet Joseph Smith speaks of this difference as recorded in the *Times and Seasons,* volume III, page 732, also same volume, page 823, first column. The "gift" is the sacred act of bestowing or conferring, or giving the Holy Ghost by the authority of the Holy Priesthood in the laying on of hands. All saints, having been baptized, who are *worthy,* receive at once the witness of the Holy Ghost, when this is given by the laying on of hands. Those who are *not* worthy, or are not prepared in spirit for the reception of the *witness,* (or the Holy Ghost) may not receive it for days, or months, or perhaps for years, and some never are blessed with the power of the baptism of the Holy Ghost at all, the seed having fallen in thorns, or on stony ground. (See the parable of the sower.) Joseph says: D&C Section 130:23, "A man may receive the Holy Ghost, and it may descend upon him and not tarry with him." That may be the case with any man, but those who are worthy, true and faithful are at all times entitled to His presence, more especially at times of need, when men are humble, putting their trust in God. When men sin, the Spirit departs from them unless they repent. But, you know all these things.

A Difficult Field of Labor

Late in 1896, Hyrum was transferred to a difficult field of labor, just south of the Scottish border, in Westoe, South Shields. In spite of a bad cold, Hyrum expressed his determination to succeed, to which Joseph F. responded:

November 12, 1896

Well, I am sorry you took such a bad cold just on reaching your new field of labor, but I hope and pray you will, by faith and prudence, soon recover from it entirely. England is a bad place for getting over a cold. I have tried it, and I hope you will never suffer as I have done there with colds. Bad colds were my worst enemies while there. But I can now see wherein I lacked judgment in taking care of myself. A day or two of rest and proper treatment, if taken in time, will often check disease in the bud, which if neglected, or dallied with, becomes serious. . . .

I am glad you feel like taking hold in your new field with courage and determination. There is nothing like a hard field of labor to try the metal and develop the spirit and faith of a young man, provided he trusts in the Lord and does not flinch from duty. Your labors are for your own as well as for others' good. See to it, my Son, that in *your* case, "One good man and the Lord Almighty are a big majority"—over all obstacles.

A Day in the Office of the First Presidency

On November 12, 1896, Joseph F. wrote Hyrum and included an outline of his day's activities. John T. Caine, who had served in the Sandwich Islands with Joseph F. Smith, had been Utah's delegate to Congress from 1883 to 1893. He was defeated in his bid to become Utah's first Democratic governor in 1895, and at the time of this letter was chairman of the Utah Senate's Committee on Appropriations. John M. Cannon, a grandson of George Q. Cannon, was a Salt Lake City lawyer, having graduated from the University of Michigan in 1890. Simon Bamberger, prominent in the Utah Jewish community, later became governor of Utah. Perry Nebeker, a bodyguard for Brigham Young during the Utah War, had served as mission president of Switzerland, Italy, France, Germany, and Holland (1863-67) and was a member of the state legislature. George C. Parkinson, president of the Oneida Stake in Idaho, was a member of Idaho's Senate. Son of Heber C. Kimball and father of Spencer W. Kimball, Andrew Kimball was released as president of the Indian Missions in 1897 and became president of the St. Joseph Stake (Arizona) the following year.

November 12, 1896

Just for fun I will give you an idea. On reaching the office we found Hon. J. T. Caine, John M. Cannon, Mr. Bamberger and a lady, and Mr. Luce there awaiting us. We listened to each in turn, and disposed of their business. Then came Perry Nebeker, George C. Parkinson, E. A. Kimball of the Southern States, and Andrew Kimball of the Indian Territory Missions. And we listened to each of these in turn and advised in all their matters, the latter two being turned over to me. Then came C. W. Penrose, who with Brother Parkinson have just gone. Each of these people had different matters of interest to them and their various concerns, which took from 15 to 40 minutes each, to state their cases. And we are supposed to listen complacently, consider well, and advise them what to do. Whoever thinks there is nothing but pleasant pastime in all this, is wide of the mark!

Writing Skills

Always alert to find ways of helping his children

improve, Joseph F. frequently pointed out spelling and grammatical errors in his sons' letters. He never forgot the disadvantages he experienced as a result of his own lack of formal education and seemed determined that his children would fare better. In his letter of December 17, 1896, Joseph F. acknowledged one of his own literary foibles and encouraged Hyrum to greater awareness of syntax and verbosity.

December 17, 1896

I know of no such word as "incidences." Incidence is all right. I do not attempt to counsel your spelling because *I* am a good speller myself, but only because I would like you to spell and write better than I. To your diction, too, I might take a little exception, if it would help you to improve in that direction. Let me say, never use two words in one sentence which practically mean the same thing, for that has been, and is one of my own failings in speaking, but not in writing, so much. Always avoid totology.

You say, "The *past* year has appeared to *pass* by very rapidly, yet the beginning of it seems a terrible long way*s* in the distance." Now this sentiment is not quite clear to me. Do you mean, "the year just past appears to have slid by rapidly, yet looking back to the beginning of it, it seemed a long way off (or in the distance)?" Or do you mean that looking to the end of the year from the beginning, it seemed a long way off?

Make your sentences, and paragraphs short and terse. And avoid a profusion of words. One of my worst faults in speaking and writing is that I make my sentences, or paragraphs too lengthy. In so doing it is hard to get at the chit or substance of the idea. For example, you say, "Were I to compare the difficulties and the troubles and the questions that must be constantly coming up before you brethren who stand at the head of so many people, with those that are continually coming before me in a little bit of a branch of the Church, I wonder how you stand it." Now my son, you see your paragraph is so long that you forgot to say what you would do or not do—"Were" you "to compare the difficulties" &c. &c. I suppose you intended to say, "Were I to compare the difficulties and troubles you have to settle, and answer the questions constantly coming up before you, who stand at the head of so many people, with such difficulties &c., as come before me in a little branch of the Church, *my troubles would appear very insignificant to those you have.*" Well, I do not find any fault. I am only pointing out some small defects which no one *more* than yourself should desire to avoid. It is common to say "some way or another," "some time or another." But it may be seen at a glance that "*some* way" means *one* way or another, or one out of many ways. "Some time," means at one time or at another time, and to add "or another" is superfluous, and in sense totological. "Some way" is equivalent to "one way or another." You will see this at a glance. Some people, and generally acknowledged to be good writers and speakers too, use the double word "subject matter," while the plain truth is that the "subject" is the "matter," and the "matter," is the "subject." Corbitt, the great grammarian, denounces this unwarranted use of two words in one, both meaning the same thing.

Joseph F.'s next letter showed that he was able to accept correction by his son and still had room for improvement.

January 23, 1897

I cheerfully acknowledge the correction in the spelling of "tautology," and can stand any amount of correction from wrong, for I would rather be right than be king. Of course, I think you will not question the fact that the lapsis was due more to thoughtlessness, or haste than to real ignorance, for the instant its incorrectness was called to my attention I knew it was wrong and how it should be spelt.

Dignity in Contention

In his letter of August 17, 1897, Hyrum related an experience that he and his companions had with a heckler at a public meeting. Rather than avoiding the confrontation, Hyrum debated and defended the teachings of the Church, but not without ridicule and harrassment from his opponent. Joseph F. took this opportunity to suggest to Hyrum the appropriate times, and with whom, a gospel discussion should or should not be debated.

September 3, 1897

I do not wish to chide you for having allowed yourself to contend . . . on a public rostrum, but I could not help feeling it was a little undignified on your part. While I approve of your efforts to defend the truth, and commend you in the exercise of vigor and holy zeal in the defense of the truth, allow me to suggest that when you are compelled by a sense of duty to meet the enemy, try and make sure that your "foe is worthy of your steel." The truth is always dignified and her advocates and defenders should carefully maintain a corresponding dignity in the choice of their associates and in yielding to come in contact with those who oppose, but I do not blame you. On the contrary, I know your heart and intentions were good and, therefore, it will be overruled eventually for good. But as far as you can, consistently, avoid street rabbles and noisy contentions, which can never be mistaken by candid people for argument or reason. It is calm reason and cold truth that will weigh in the balance. Seek to convey the truths you utter with moderate voice, without excitement, deliberately, and as well chosen words as you can possibly command. You will then, as Disraeli did, command the attention of your auditors, and not only that, but their respect.

Thoughts of Returning Home

As Hyrum neared the two-year mark of his mission, he began to have thoughts of returning home. He mentioned plans he was making for his return and was understandably looking forward to reunion with his wife and family. Joseph F. wisely counseled his son to work hard to the end and not to anticipate his release from the mission field. Events proved this to be good advice, for Hyrum's call was extended briefly to further assist the mission president.

In one of his last letters to Hyrum on this mission, Joseph F. offered further advice to help his son in the transition to Church service at home.

September 25, 1897

Bro. D____ begins to think that his time in England is drawing very short, and that from this [time] on he would be pardoned for looking towards home. I do not object to this in the least, provided he does not allow his looking toward home to interfere in the least with his continued faithfulness in the ministry, and I would say the same to you. Do not get in a hurry, be patient in your labors and abide your time, and do not make up your mind that the time is set for your release. If you do, and you should not be released at the precise time you expect, it will be a very great disappointment to you, and the time thereafter . . . might drag very heavily on your hands. Rather, make up your mind to remain until the Lord and your brethren are satisfied with your labors, or until your release shall come. You will then be subjected to no disappointments.

November 11, 1897

We will welcome you home anytime, and so far as we

are concerned the sooner the better. But I earnestly desire that you will never, through all your life, throw off the armor of the Gospel, or cease to advocate, defend and practice the precepts of the Son of God. I want you to be faithful, to complete your mission, to abide your time, and when God's servants shall say it is enough for this time, to come home with spotless garments and a clear conscience. Nothing could grieve me more than to think you would not do all this, and nothing could give me more joy and satisfaction [than] to know you will come home pure and unspotted from the world. I have all confidence in your integrity. I believe in you with all my heart, and I love you with all my soul. I pray for you always. My thoughts of you in your labors are a constant prayer for your success. I do not believe in flattery. I prize real merit. And, therefore, I am grateful and pleased with every kind word I hear spoken of you by others. I know, as a boy, you possessed good sense and a good share of wisdom. As a *man* I am sure you cannot but be a *man* of *principle* and of noble impulses, a man of true and noble heart and soul. I look to you for counsel and moral support. I rely upon you as my first son—bone of my bone and flesh of my flesh. I cannot forsake you and I ask you to cleave to me and your mother with filial love, and I know you will. Not only so, but should anything happen to me I shall expect you to honor me by impartial consideration of all my family. I believe your nature inclines to judgment and impartial justice, and also to mercy and forgiveness. To have my sons disagree and pull apart would wound me to the core. I want my family to agree to be united and my children to be *one*. God bless you now and forever and when released honorably, bring you safely home.

December 26, 1897

I am *pleased* rather than sorry that President R. S. Wells is in no hurry to dispense with your labors and to send you home. I consider this fact the highest compliment he has paid you, and it is an *honor*, to be thus appreciated, of which both you and I may well be pleased. How much better it is to be in *demand*, than to be *in* the *way*. Or I might better say, how desirable it is so to live and labor in the fields assigned us, that our file-leaders and associates will be satisfied with what we do. I tell Buddie, Alvin and Joseph F. that the thing for them to do is, *if possible,* to make themselves and their services to their employers, not only desirable but *indispensible!* Then their prosperity is assured. Of course, we would have been glad to see you sooner but our joy on your return will be none the less for your longer stay, in as much as your labors were longer needed, and at last you return "pure and unspotted from the world." Nor will you lose anything in the end by such detention.

Joseph R. and Joseph Fielding (1899-1901)

While Hyrum M. was laboring in England, Joseph Richards (son of Sarah) and Joseph Fielding, Jr. (son of Julina), were preparing for their missions. Joseph R. (also called "Richards," or "Buddie") worked in the ZCMI drug department, making twenty-five dollars a month. Joseph Fielding attended school, married Louie Shurtliff on April 26, 1898, and began working in the ZCMI grocery department.

In September 1898, Wilford Woodruff passed away, and Lorenzo Snow was sustained as President of the Church with George Q. Cannon and Joseph F. Smith as Counselors. To relieve the Church's indebtedness, the First Presidency decided to issue a million dollars in bonds, to be redeemed in seven years.

After a prolonged period of intense work, Joseph F. took a two-month vacation to Hawaii with his wife Sarah and two daughters. Two months after their return, Joseph R. and Joseph Fielding left on their missions to Great Britain, arriving in early June 1899.

The year 1900 was particularly strenuous for Joseph F. In January, Elder B. H. Roberts was denied his seat as Utah's elected representative to the U.S. House of Representatives because he was a polygamist. Soon afterward, President Cannon was partially paralyzed, and President Snow was confined to his bed much of the time. Consequently, the burden of the First Presidency fell upon the shoulders of Joseph F., who traveled to Mexico and Canada, visiting recently established colonies there, and often worked late into the night to keep up with his correspondence.

In April 1901, President Cannon passed away. Joseph R. and Joseph Fielding were released from their missions in June, and President Smith traveled to Boston to meet them.

Obtaining a Testimony

Immediately upon arriving in England, Joseph R. wrote his father two letters expressing reservations about his testimony and raising questions about his effectiveness as a missionary. Anxious to bolster his son's faltering faith, Joseph F. responded with an expression of love and reminded him of God's love and every individual's privilege of choice. Finally, he reassured Joseph R. that commensurate with his own dedication and sincerity, the Lord would strengthen his testimony.

June 20, 1899

It was with feelings of great joy mingled with sadness that we received your favors of the 4th and 5th inst. . . . We pray for you earnestly and most sincerely desire that you may humble yourself, obtain the spirit of your calling and of the ministry to which you have been sent, that you may be instrumental in the hands of the Lord of not only convincing yourself of the truths of the Gospel of everlasting life, but that you may be instrumental in bringing others to a knowledge of the same. It is for these reasons you have been called and sent forth, and I esteem the good which may result to you through your obedience to the call, and your effort to fulfill it honorably as being of greater consequence to me and to your mother, and above all, to yourself, than to any other living creature, although you might succeed in bringing many to the knowledge of the Gospel. If you can see, by the prompting of the Holy Spirit, and also by the prompting of your own judgment that the world is in sin and in transgression of the laws of God, then it should follow that the world ought to be warned of the consequences of sin and be taught to return to the laws of God and to works of righteousness, and blessed indeed is he who may be the instrument in the hand of the Lord of bringing even one soul out of darkness into the light, and out of the bonds of iniquity into the marvelous liberty of the Gospel.

Christ rules by the principle of love; God's method of ruling is by that of love, and upon the principle of intelligence he has given us our agency, he has set before us, practically speaking, the tree of knowledge of good and of evil, and in the Gospel he has pointed out to us the glorious consequences of obedience to the laws of righteousness, the partaking of the good fruit of the tree of knowledge, and of the dreadful consequences of partaking of the fruit of evil of its tree. And having pointed out the consequences, he leaves us free as individuals to choose our own course. In the language of the poet, as you will find in the hymn book, "Know this, that every soul is free, to choose his course and what he'll be; for this eternal truth is given, that God will force no man to heaven. He'll call, persuade, direct him right, bless him with wisdom, love and light; in nameless ways be good and kind, but never force the human mind."

I would call your attention to the 82nd section of the Doctrine and Covenants, paragraph four; also paragraphs five to ten, and I pray you to remember these words: "I the Lord am bound when ye do what I say. But when ye do not what I say, ye have no promise." It will do no good to fast or pray unless it is with a sincere and earnest desire in the heart to learn the will of the Lord with an unalterable determination to do it. . . .

May God bless you my boy and help you, and preserve you from the fear of the world, and help you to overcome your own timidity and to find out God, to know him, and Jesus Christ whom He hath sent into the world, whom to know is life eternal.

With love and hope, and abiding faith, I am, Affectionately, your father,
Jos. F. Smith
[P.S.] My own Dear Son: I had to close at this point in order to attend a meeting. . . . I know it was and is the *will* of God, our Heavenly Father that you should take this mission. And it is His will that you should succeed, but it is your duty to see and acknowledge His hand therein and to do your best to meet His will and purpose concerning it. It is also *my will, nay more,* my *earnest desire* and my *hope,* my *faith* and most *fervent prayer* to God, my Father, that you shall succeed in this mission. . . . You must not fail! And you will not, no you cannot fail, if you will but do your duty. My God, bless and help my son! Think of us. Ever. Papa.

Various Admonitions and a Promise

It was Joseph F. Smith's practice to write separate letters to both of his missionary sons, usually on the same day. Though the letters often contained the same news of home, they were always personalized for the benefit of each son. Thus, on the day Joseph F. wrote Joseph R. (Buddie), encouraging him to obtain a stronger testimony of the gospel and his mission, he wrote Joseph Fielding a letter containing several admonitions, including a reminder to write his wife Louie, and a promise.

June 20, 1899

I am glad to hear that the people of the ship treated you kindly and that you did not see any occasion to find fault with anything except the slow progress of the voyage.

As for scoffing unbelievers, it is not worth your while to waste time or the energy of your thought on them. Let your mind turn as it naturally does upon the duties of your mission and calling. Do not stop to trouble yourself about what the world may think of you, or what enemies may say about you. Of one thing be sure, that is, that you are in fellowship with the Almighty, and have a conscience void of offence towards all men. Do not seek to excel men, only seek to do your duty faithfully and well, leaving all the results in the hands of the Lord. It will then be well with you both in time and in eternity. . . .

There is nothing that could give me more joy and satisfaction than the realization which I have that you possess the spirit of the Gospel and have received the testimony of its truth. God bless you forever in this regard, my son, and cause you to develop in mind and to grow in understanding and in the knowledge of His truth until you shall know as you are known and see as you are seen. And withal, I admonish you to use judgment and cultivate patience and humility; be not censorious or arbitrary, rather be yielding and humble in your spirit and assert the truth by moral suasion and gentle fervor than by dogmatic force. Write as often as you can, not to interfere with your duties. A good letter to me will be one to all the family except Louie, who will expect to have her own correspondence from you. We want her to feel that your home is not broken up. Your rooms are at her service and command at any moment, and she is welcome to come and occupy them whenever and as long as she pleases. . . . She is a good girl, and we confidently expect the Lord will bless her and you so that you both shall accomplish a glorious mission in all its fulness on the earth, and I don't want either of you to feel the least discouraged in any possible way, but to continue to put your trust in the Lord and he will most assuredly open your way. I feel so confident in my spirit in making this promise that I would almost pronounce it an inspired prediction, but never

63

mind, we will trust in the Lord and we feel sure that He will do all things right.

Safety in Companionship

In late September 1899, Joseph F. returned from a trip to Oregon to find a letter from Joseph Fielding. Anti-Mormon sentiment in England was at fever pitch. Malicious rumors and slanders were being circulated that the missionaries were in England to entice British girls away from their homes and ship them off to Utah where they would be coerced into polygamous relations. False and sensational stories spread like wildfire among the gullible, some of whom became so incensed as to resort to violence to oppose the "Mormon menace." Joseph Fielding described one such scene, to which his father responded.

September 27, 1899

I was very sorry that you have been subjected to such an unmerciful siege of mobbing in that boasted land of freedom and equal rights. I hope you will be very cautious to avoid such hornets' nests of anti-Mormonism and hatred and viciousness on the part of the Jarmanites or anybody else. While it is evident the adversary is afraid of some good being done in such places it is well not to invite such treatment if you can reasonably avoid it. I am sincerely thankful that you escaped without injury, and pray that God will always deliver you from the wrath of the wicked. It is always prudent, under such circumstances, and as a general thing, to keep together. One should never travel alone. The Lord has provided that the elders should travel two and two, and there should never be less than two of you together. Mamma was considerably worried after she read your letter for she feels that you are the apple of her eye and if turned loose on those that would molest you she would scarcely leave a grease spot of them.

The Voice of Warning and Testimony

Throughout Joseph F. Smith's life, the most intense and persistent opposition to the Church came from Protestant ministers. Clergymen often led the mobs in Missouri and Illinois. During his missions to Hawaii and England, ministers actively campaigned against the Church, often, through ignorance or malice, spreading false reports about its history and doctrine. During the 1870s and 1880s, Protestant missionary societies established ninety free schools in Utah, hoping to win Latter-day Saint children away from the faith of their parents through "education." In 1898, when Elder B. H. Roberts of the First Council of Seventy was elected Utah's representative to the U. S. House of Representatives, the Salt Lake Ministerial Association protested. Petitions protesting the seating of Roberts were circulated in churches throughout the country, eventually gathering seven million signatures.

On December 8, 1899, Joseph F. wrote Buddie, "I think Congress will oust Hon. B. H. Roberts. But if so, it will be a blot upon the House of Representatives and upon the nation. I'll venture to guess there is not another man in Congress, save it may be Rawlins [Utah's Senator], who is as clean and free from taint of crime as he. If ousted it will be by the force of sectarian cant and hypocrisy, simon pure!" Primarily through the efforts of hostile clergymen, the House denied Roberts his seat within days of the following letter to Joseph Fielding.

In spite of the animosity frequently encountered from ministers of the time, Joseph F. counseled his son to be respectful, and leave his testimony with them. The advice not to tarry long with unresponsive contacts is as relevant today as it was eighty years ago.

January 2, 1900

It gives me pleasure to acknowledge the receipt of

your esteemed favors of December 2nd and 18th, the first of which reached me December 19th, and the latter this morning. I am pleased to say that it gives me pleasure to read your letters and to discern as I do between the lines the excellent spirit which pervades your thoughts and accompanies you in your ministrations. I was interested in your communications to the reverend gentleman you name in reference to the principles of the Gospel, and while it is all right to get after those gentlemen in the true spirit of inquiry and of hope of enlightening them, it is always well to be brief and pointed and courteous in such communications, as I think you have been. As a rule, the more you say to such people, the more opportunity is given to them for criticism and fault-finding. It is very seldom that gentlemen of *the cloth,* whose living depends upon their ecclesiastical position, will listen to reason or will yield to the persuasions of the good Spirit. They are blinded by the spirit of the world, and the profits of their calling. Besides they are thoroughly committed to their profession, for it is but a profession with them. Much labor and pains may be bestowed without good effects upon that class of people, still it is consistent and proper that they should receive admonition and warning and the testimony of the servants of the Lord, which should always be given in great humility and then they should be left in the hands of the Lord.

Receiving Praise

On December 21, 1899, Frank J. Cannon, son of President George Q. Cannon and a former senator from Utah, wrote Joseph F. Smith, reporting the favorable impression Joseph Fielding was making as a missionary in England. Joseph F. was, of course, very pleased, and passed the compliment on to his son, taking occasion to teach a valuable lesson on receiving praise.

January 5, 1900

[Quoting Frank J. Cannon's letter to Joseph F.]
"The other day while taking lunch with the countess
of Warwick, it was a pleasure to hear her speak in the
highest terms of your son Joseph, whose labors in
Warwickshire have come to her attention. Lady Warwick
recounted the facts of a marvelous case of the healing
of one of her old dependents, under Joseph's
ministrations, and she seems to be quite pleased to have her
people investigate our cause. She sent a note inviting
Joseph to come to the castle to visit with us, but
unfortunatcly hc had left the village for some other part
of the conference. Lady Warwick is a good woman who
spends her life and her wealth in noble works, and her
expressions of regard for your son and his work were quite
sincere."

I wrote a few lines to brother Cannon in
acknowledgment of his kindly mention of you, and
regretted that you had failed to receive the invitation to
lunch at the castle with her ladyship and brother and
sister Cannon. Of course we are always pleased to hear
kind words from friends relative to our boys, and we
sincerely hope you and Richards may always merit the
kind things said of you, and yet we would have you so live
and act without regard to what may be said, that your lives
and labors may be worthy of you and of the cause you are
called to represent. We must always remember that we are
not laboring for the applause of men, nor to gain favors
which we do not deserve. We need care nothing for the
opinions of others so long as we have a consciousness of
well-doing. Let our aim always be to do right because it
is right and because it is our mission to do good, and
leave the result in the hands of the Lord. Still it is pleasant
to be kindly thought of and to be held in the esteem of
honorable men.

Doctrinal Questions

Joseph Richards continued to be challenged by difficult doctrinal problems and frequently asked his father's opinion. Joseph F. always responded, often at great length. These letters, frequently four or more pages in length, are in Joseph F.'s handwriting, suggesting he spent much time each week writing his missionary sons. He often wrote out scriptural references which are only cited here. In this letter, Joseph F. carefully examined the questions posed by his son and then added a reminder that apparent doctrinal problems are often due more to the approach taken than to actual scriptural inconsistency.

January 6, 1900

[Quoting Richards's question.] "Whether the sons of perdition will be privileged to retain their bodies after the resurrection, or whether they will be resurrected or not?" First, yes. They will doubtless be resurrected. Second, yes. They will without doubt retain their bodies. First see D&C 29:26, 27. This means *all* the dead shall be raised from the dead. Again see Alma 11:43, 44, Revelation 20:11-15, I Corinthians 15:21-23. Second, Mosiah 16:11, D&C 29:27-28, Alma 11:45, 34:34. . . . I would like you to get clearly into your mind what the Lord has said about the second death, and what the second death is. Some believe it means the dissolution of the spirit and body after resurrection. That is impossible if the Book of Mormon and D&C are true, and I say let them be true, and let God be true though all men prove to be liars. D&C 29:41 tells us precisely what the second death is, viz., banishment from the kingdom and presence of God into outer darkness. [Alma 42:9, D&C 75:28-29, 39 are also quoted.]

It is a good rule to interpret a passage of scripture which is not clear by another or others bearing on the same or a similar subject, which may be clear and pointed. All truth is reasonable, if we can only comprehend it. I judge the things I do not know by those I do know, which bear resemblance, or relationship. To my mind there is no conflict between the command of God, "Thou shalt not kill," and his further command, that "Whosoever sheddeth man's blood, *by man shall his blood be shed.*" Both are right and both are just and true. But some people carp about it and condemn the Lord for what seems to them a contradiction. The contradiction is only in their minds.

The Book of Mormon as a Missionary Tool

In March 1900, Joseph Fielding wrote to his father, observing the importance of a knowledge of modern scriptures in the mission field. Joseph F. responded with this letter which emphasizes the role of the Book of Mormon as a missionary tool.

April 3, 1900

I note your remarks in relation to reading the Book of Mormon and the Doctrine and Covenants, and I heartily approve of your views. No man can be an efficient missionary of this church unless he is familiar with these books. And the more familiar he is with them, the more capable will he be to discharge the duties of his ministry. Indeed, I think sometimes that we neglect too much the advocacy of the Book of Mormon. In the early days of the church, it was the preaching of the Book of Mormon and the proof of its existence or coming forth, as found in the Bible, that made converts to the church. It was as necessary then to prove our authority by the Bible as it is now, but it seems to me that to show the world from the Bible that the Book of Mormon, or such a book as it is, was to come forth in the latter days, is a strong argument for our cause. It is a great mistake to set aside or ignore the word of God as revealed in the latter days in preaching this gospel to the

world. Of course it is not always wise to feed the people with
strong meat at first, but one of the foundation stones of the
church in the latter day is the revelation of the Book of
Mormon and the restoration of the Gospel it contains, as
also the visions and revelations given to the Prophet Joseph
Smith. To be ashamed of these is to be ashamed of our
ministry, to dodge these facts is to fail in the spirit of our
ministry. In my opinion these things should be preached
and then substantiated by the accepted version of the old
Bible.

Satan and Human Weakness

As he observed human behavior, Joseph Fielding won-
dered about the nature of evil and its source. He asked his
father whether Satan was the sole source of evil and to what
extent Satan was restricted from sacred places, such as the
temple. An avid student of Church history, even at this early age, Joseph Fielding knew that once, during the apostasy
at Kirtland, a number of disgruntled members tried to take
over the Church. In a meeting at the Kirtland Temple in
late 1837, Brigham Young vigorously defended Joseph
Smith. A scuffle ensued, during which some minor damage
was done to the temple. Joseph Fielding cited the incident
in his question regarding Satan's influence and human
agency.

April 3, 1900

You ask, Can a man do any wrong without first being
tempted of Satan? All men have their agency, the spirit
of Satan leads to error and darkness and wrong doing. If a
man does wrong, it is because he yields to the spirit of evil,
thereby exercising his agency. If he does good, it is in
accordance with the spirit that is of God, and he uses his
agency in that as well. Those who overcome evil in this
life will be beyond the power of Satan in the life to come.

In other words, Satan's power ends in this world so far as the righteous are concerned, for they arise above him and above his influence; and power is not given to him to tempt them in the spirit world, they having overcome him in this. So far then as the righteous are concerned, Satan is effectually bound, whether it is in this life or in the life to come. But as mortality is never free from its own weaknesses there is no perfect safety in this sphere without the presence continually of the influence of the Holy Spirit. Satan can enter any place where he is invited or permitted to enter by man. If wicked men enter the house of God or have dominion in it, Satan will have access there, but where the righteous rule and the righteousness of God prevails, there Satan cannot come, at least with power.

You ask the question, Can a man do wrong in the temple if Satan is not there to urge him on? In the case you cite with reference to the Kirtland Temple it would seem that Satan himself had taken possession of the minds of those men, and if not in the temple in person, his power was certainly manifested through his agents there, who were apostates. I repeat, Satan, by his presence or power, can go anywhere that man can go who invites him or yields to him and his influence. The prevalence of the spirit of apostasy on the occasion you refer to gave the adversary almost full control at that time in the temple, and it is only by the power of righteousness that Satan and his influence was expelled therefrom. As to whether the binding of Satan is a literal binding as with a chain or not, it matters not. I am inclined to believe that the chain spoken of in the Bible, with which Satan is to be bound, is more figurative than real. He will be bound both by the faith of the righteous and the decrees of the Almighty during the Millennial reign and will be cast down into hell, as the prophets have said, and shall not be at liberty to molest the children of men until the end of the thousand years. . . .

As to the agency of man, it is by the light of Christ and

71

the power of God that man by his agency can become exalted through obedience to the laws of God. It is by his agency that he becomes a son of perdition after having received the truth, by yielding again himself to the power of Satan. A man who by his agency conquers Satan, subdues the evil that is in him, and rises above the power of temptation and of all evil, is still as much a free agent as he was when he was subject to temptation, but then he is like God or Christ, beyond the power of evil.

Partakers of the Sacrament

When the missionary presiding over the conference to which Joseph R. had been assigned was released and returned to Utah, he reported to Joseph F. On July 27, 1901, Joseph F. wrote Joseph R. that "he spoke very kindly of you and said that not only he but all the boys in the mission held you in very high esteem." Always endeavoring to strengthen his knowledge and testimony of the gospel, Joseph R. was said to be "a good student" who was always "trying to improve." He continued to carefully examine the scriptures and history of the church. In this case, he discovered an apparent discrepancy regarding partakers of the sacrament. Joseph F. responded.

February 8, 1901

Now, about administering the Sacrament to new converts. If you will read carefully Section 20, paragraph 68, Doctrine and Covenants, I think you will see that you have not quite understood it. The head line, commencing verse 68, viz: "The duty of the members after they are received by baptism" is but a caption to all the verses which follow to the end of the section, and stands apart from the instructions which follow. Read verse 68 without reference to the caption, or head line. "The Elders or Priests (who baptize) are to have a sufficient time to expound *all things* concerning the Church of Christ to their understanding previous to their partaking of the Sacrament and being confirmed by the laying on of hands etc." "Expound all things." Baptism should be expounded as well as confirmation and partaking of the Sacrament before they (the converts) are either baptized, confirmed, or partake of the Sacrament. Baptism is part of the "all things," which is as necessary to expound to their understanding before they receive it as either of the other ordinances referred to. The Sacrament is for members of the church in good standing. Membership consists of belief and faith, repentance, baptism by immersion by authority, and confirmation and the gift of the Holy Ghost by the laying on of hands. Jesus did not institute the Sacrament for non-members or unbelievers, nor for mere seekers after the truth but for those "*in* the covenant." See Matt. 26:26; Mark 14:22; Luke 22:19; 1st Cor. 11:23-31. "This do ye in remembrance of me." See Book of Mormon, 3rd Nephi, 18:11: "And this shall ye always do to those who repent and are baptized in my name, etc." Confirmation follows baptism. Verse 5: "Behold there shall be one ordained among you and to him will I give power, etc." "and bless it, and give it unto the people of *my church*, unto all those who shall believe and *be baptized* in my name." They are not of "my church" or members until confirmed. "That ye shall not suffer any one knowingly to partake of my flesh unworthily etc." See the whole chapter. . . . The Sacrament is for those who are *members* of the body of Christ, i.e., members of the church.

The extract from the Prophet's History, published in the Manual 1899-1900, page 53, Note 2, squarely states that the "two sisters" were confirmed after they partook of the Sacrament. If this is true, it was no doubt an error or an oversight. This was done in September 1830, five months after the first organization of the church with six members. Joseph was young in the work and may not *then* have known or sensed fully the true order of things.

It may have been in a measure like the first baptisms for the dead. When that principle was first revealed it was so new and yet so glorious, that without further light the saints rushed into the river at Nauvoo and were baptized, men for women and women for men, i.e., a man would be baptized for his father and mother, his brothers and sisters, etc., and women were baptized for their fathers, mothers, etc. But soon the Lord revealed the principle more fully. (See D&C 127 and 128.) Joseph and the people then learned that baptism for the dead must be performed in the temple in a font prepared and dedicated for that purpose. And men should act for men, and women for women. And thus the church was taught and learned "here a little, and there a little, line upon line, and precept upon precept." But there is an error in the quotation from the history; it says, "Newel Knight and his wife paid us a visit at my place at Harmony, Pennsylvania, and as neither *his wife nor himself* had been as yet confirmed, etc." Then it says, "After which we confirmed *these two sisters,*" which is a manifest error, for Newel Knight and his wife could not have been "these two sisters." I have taken pains to hunt this up in the Original Manuscript History. And there it reads as follows: "Neither Emma nor Sister Knight had been confirmed," etc. The rest is correctly given. The true order is to administer the Sacrament to members only and *not* to *them* if they are unworthy.

Keeping a Journal

From the age of fifteen, when he began his first mission, Joseph F. Smith kept a daily journal. Throughout his life he referred to his journal to obtain valuable information and impressions that would have been lost had he not been so careful to keep a personal record. As recent prophets have done, Joseph F. urged missionaries, including Joseph Fielding, to keep a daily diary.

February 20, 1901

Always take time to eat your meals and post your journal. I have had experience in these matters. A diary is almost worthless unless written daily. We cannot journalize correctly from *memory*. Keep your diary up.

Death of a Daughter

In February 1901, Joseph R.'s seventeen-year-old sister Alice reached the point of exhaustion after a prolonged period of intense studying. She had often studied into the small hours of the morning. Against her father's advice, she persisted until she became seriously ill. In spite of medical attention and the faith and prayers of the entire family, "Alibo" died on April 29. Joseph F. immediately sent word to his missionary sons and two weeks later expressed his grief to Joseph R. As this letter makes clear, only his faith in the Lord and the knowledge that Alibo would be with them in the resurrection sustained the prophet during this time of great loss. Sarah had previously lost three other children.

May 14, 1901

Your welcome letter of April 30th has just come to hand. Your letter was written just one day after our Darling "Alibo's" death. It came to my hand today. And I suppose my brief note to you of April 29th will have reached you yesterday or today, conveying to you and to Joseph F. the sad news of our irreparable earthly loss. Our hearts are still bowed down in the earth where the remains of our sweet girl and those of her little Brothers and Sisters repose in the dust. The blow was hard upon all of us, but it fell with mighty force upon the frail of her beloved and precious Mother. May the merciful Father sustain and preserve the mortal life of our darling "Mamma." She is not strong at best, and this crucial ordeal has drawn heavily upon the little she had. But we will do the best we can, by the help of the Lord, and from our hearts we feel that our sleeping treasures are all in His holy keeping and will soon awake from dust to immortality and eternal life. But for the precious assurance and hope in the Gospel of Christ, life would not only *not* be worth the living, but it would be an infamous and damning *farce*! But, "O, what joy this sentence gives, I *know* that *my Redeemer lives*!" Thank God. He is "the resurrection and the life," and his word is true. "He that believeth in me, tho he were dead, yet shall he live; and whosoever liveth and believeth in me shall *never die*."

To Joseph Fielding, Joseph F. wrote:

She knew no sin against God or man. Too good, it seems, to live in this poor sin-cursed world. And so the good Father who gave her to us, has taken her to himself again. We shall meet again "beyond the river where the surges cease to roll." O! what happifying thought! She came to us under the Holy Bond of the New and everlasting Covenant. Whosoever God hath joined together neither man, nor time, nor distance, nor even death can sever. How grateful I am for God's truth and power unto salvation.

Alvin F., H. Chase, George C., and Willard R. (1905-1907)

President Lorenzo Snow passed away October 10, 1901. Seven days later, Joseph F. was set apart as President of the Church, with John R. Winder and Anthon H. Lund as counselors. On October 24, Hyrum M. Smith was called to the apostleship and sustained as a member of the Quorum of the Twelve.

One high priority of President Smith's administration was the redemption of the Church's million-dollar bond issue. On New Year's Eve, 1903, the First Presidency celebrated the half-way mark in paying off the bonds. But their satisfaction was restrained by the knowledge that in a few days the U.S. Senate's Committee on Privileges and Elections would begin hearing to consider protests against the seating of Apostle Reed Smoot. Allegations had been made that the Church continued to encourage polygamy and controlled Utah politics, and that Smoot's position as an Apostle had compromised his allegiance to the United States. Subpoenaed to testify, President Smith traveled to Washington and submitted to four days of grueling examination in March 1904. Returning for April conference, he reiterated that the practice of plural marriage had been officially discontinued since 1890 and declared that any members violating the Manifesto would be excommunicated.

As the Smoot hearings continued, newspapers and

magazines throughout the country reprinted sensational charges made by the *Salt Lake Tribune*. Through the inflammatory editorials of George Q. Cannon's disaffected son, Frank J., the *Tribune* heaped abuse on President Smith, severely trying his Christian spirit.

In the midst of this uproar four of Joseph F.'s sons were sent on missions: Alvin Fielding (son of Edna), Heber Chase (son of Alice), Willard Richards (son of Sarah), and George Carlos (son of Julina). At thirty, Alvin was the oldest, and Willard, nineteen, the youngest. Alvin, George, and Chase left wives and children at home.

They left for England on April 19, 1905, where they received their assignments from European mission president Heber J. Grant: Alvin to London; George to Sundsvall, Sweden; Chase to Cheltenham, England; and Willard to Trondheim, Norway.

In December, Joseph F. and a trainload of Church and state dignitaries traveled to Vermont for the dedication of the Joseph Smith Memorial at the Prophet's birthplace. Apostles John W. Taylor and Matthias F. Cowley had submitted their resignations to the Quorum of the Twelve, confessing they were unable to abide the official interpretation of the Manifesto. But the resignations were not announced until the following April Conference.

During the summer of 1906, Joseph F. and his wife Edna and their close friend Charles W. Nibley made a tour of Europe. It was the first time a President of the Church had visited Europe, and Joseph F. took advantage of the tour to visit with his sons in London. In the fall, Charles W. Penrose replaced Elder Grant as mission president.

In November 1906, the anti-Mormon element in Salt Lake City attracted media attention by charging Joseph F. with a violation of the "unlawful cohabitation" statute, which law enforcement officials had generally ignored. Pleading guilty, Joseph F. was fined three hundred dollars and released. But the hopes of the Mormon-haters were dashed when, on February 20, 1907, the U.S. Senate, after three years of hearings, voted in favor of Reed Smoot retaining his seat. The Church and its leaders had been vindicated. And the Church was free of debt, the last of the bonds being redeemed on December 31, 1906.

In the spring of 1907, the four sons in Europe were released. Joseph F. sent their brothers Joseph Fielding and David A. to meet them in Boston and show them the new memorial in Vermont and other Church history sites on the way home. They arrived in Salt Lake City on June 11, 1907. In December, David A. was called to the Presiding Bishopric as a counselor to Bishop Charles W. Nibley.

Remedy for Homesickness

While Willard was en route to his assignment in Norway, Joseph F. wrote, offering some advice on how best to alleviate the homesickness common to many missionaries at the beginning of their ministry.

May 20, 1905

I hope your voyage across the German ocean was not unpleasant, and that you reached your destination in perfect safety. You must not forget President Grant's recipe for home sickness—"Work, work, WORK!" Pitch in and learn the language. You will find that the Scandinavians are generally a good people. And I know the Saints in those countries will be kind to my boys. We are anxious to hear from you since your arrival at your destination.

Gratitude for Family

Three of the four sons who served missions together left wives and, in some cases, children at home. Joseph F. took a great interest in his daughters-in-law and grandchildren, keeping in close contact with them and passing on family news to the missionaries. In this letter, Joseph F. described his feelings of gratitude for his large and increasing family.

May 26, 1905

The fact is, I think my grandchildren from first to last are among the very nicest and best that were ever born into this world of ours. All perfect, in body, and mind, without a single blemish or spot. Oh! how good and kind the Lord has been to me and mine in this regard! Who can measure the gratitude I feel to Him for all His merciful kindness to me? No tongue can tell or words portray my soul's full gratitude to Him for all I have received from His gracious, loving hand. Good and true children, devoted loving Mothers and wives; enough to eat and drink and wear, and where to lay our heads in peace. My Son, for all of these I thank my Heavenly Father, and rejoice in the glorious Savior of my soul. How can we help but love and be loyal to the giver of so much?

Unpleasant Experiences Are Valuable

Arriving in Norway, Willard R. described some unpleasant experiences he had encountered in lands that were, to him, strange and foreign. Joseph F. wisely and humorously pointed out that even unpleasant experiences are to be valued.

May 26, 1905

So you did not enjoy the smell of paint and bilge-water of the boats, nor the atmosphere of the boxcars of England and the continent. And you never before smelt a smell that smelt like that smell smelt! Well, if you had been in the "hold" or in the forecastle, or stearage, no doubt you would have smelt that smell more profusely than you did. In all of those places I have smelt it intensified many fold by tobacco smoke from sailors, nasty pipes, and the aroma from the stalls of the beef cattle and mutton sheep, and poultry, carried for the use of the passengers. Now they carry all these things in refrigerators, dressed ready for the cook's galley. Things have changed since I was a boy and crossed the seas with the divine message you bear. Experience is better possessed than to be gained. I.e., it is like the hurt of a bruise. It feels better after it quits hurting.

Use of Means

Though he had saved money for his mission, George C.'s funds were limited, particularly since he had left a wife and baby at home. He evidently expressed concern at the financial burden the four missionaries were imposing on their father. Joseph F.'s response revealed the priorities he set for his means.

May 28, 1905

In the first place, I will say, all I have in this world has come to me through the kind providence of the Lord. And such means as I can command for uses outside of the support of my family cannot be better used than for the support of my sons in the mission field.

It is true I have nothing to throw away. I have a very large family to maintain . . . besides many charities I have to meet. But I propose to help my boys to fill honorable missions, and while I have the means, you shall not be left without your actual necessities. Do not fear for the care of your loved ones at home. They will be taken care of, and will not lack for anything that we have the power or means to supply them, to the extent of their needs. If the Lord will bless them with wisdom and health to guard against hurtful exposures, there will be no cause for you to worry one moment about them.

Field of Labor

Now about your going to Sundsvall. I rather think it was a good stroke of policy to send you there. It would not be wise to show one of my boys any preference or favor. You have gone out to do missionary duty, not to hunt "snaps" nor to "see sights." Let everyone stand, or rise or fall upon real merit. Do your duty without a murmur, or a "kick" and show such an example of integrity and true devotion to duty and to the cause of truth, that your light will shine out, undimn'd and untarnished by selfishness or reluctance to meet what comes. I want my boys to avoid, absolutely the manifestation of a feeling or thought expressed in the aphorism, "I am better than thou!" Better *is* as better *does.* . . .

Stick to your post. If it is a hard one the more you will enjoy a change to a better one. If my boys shrink from hard work or hard fields, others will have more excuse for doing so. If you take what comes without complaint, you will set a good example to others.

Rewards

He that does well, will not lose his reward, and he who does better than another, or than others, and boasts not of it, nor prides himself on his superior works will surely receive *his* reward. And it will be a glorious one. Remember our gracious Savior. He excelled all men, in all things good and great. Yet He took not the honor to Himself. The honor, the glory, the power and the dominion He ascribed to God, the Father! He came not to do His own will, but the will of Him that sent Him. He said that while the foxes had holes and birds of the air had nests, He had not where to lay His head. Yet He did not complain nor murmur. He was on His Father's business and He knew from whom and how His reward would come. Remember the battle is not assured to the strong nor the race to the swift, but to him who endures to the end, and is most skillful in the use of his powers. It is the meek who are to inherit the earth. The peacemakers who shall be called the children of God. . . . Be tractable and teachable that you may the better teach others. One who will not be taught or will not learn good things from others is not fit to assume the role of an instructor.

Brevity and Clarity

Anxious for his sons to excel in every undertaking, Joseph F. frequently counseled his sons in the art of letter writing, since a mission was also an opportunity to acquire skills of expression that would help them throughout their lives. In this letter, brevity and clarity were recommended to George C.

May 25, 1905

You will remember the apology so often quoted for long letters, "Excuse this long, rambling letter, for I have not the time to make it shorter." True oratory is nothing more than simple, clear-cut, intelligent expression. Spread-eagle-ism, verbosity, a "diarrhea of words," can never be counted as oratory. The best language, is simple language. The most effective expression is to say what we mean and mean what we say, and as near as possible to the point. The true purpose of language is to convey our real, true meaning, to the understanding of others.

Courage, Seeking the Spirit, and Self-Control

Alvin F.'s recital of his first street meetings reminded Joseph F. of similar trials he experienced in England. He encouraged Alvin to continued effort and counseled him to obtain the Spirit for best results. Candidly admitting that a quick temper was his own worst enemy, Joseph F. advised Alvin to "keep cool in the moment of excitement or trial."

June 8, 1905

You speak of street meetings. I can realize your feelings with regard to that matter, for I have been "thro' the mill." I never did relish the opening or beginning of open air or street meetings, but I faced the music, and when I got well engaged the fear would leave me, and I would rather enjoy it. In Hull, Yorkshire, we used to take our stand by King William's monument, and first attract as many as we could by *singing*. Then we would open up on the crowd, the best we could. In Sheffield, we would go down by the market. In Leeds at "Hunslets Lane," and other places, and in Liverpool, before St. George's Hall. I have held forth on Glasgow green and many other places. But I never went into the streets, or highways or byways to speak, or *try* to speak, to moving crowds without feeling that sense of uncertainty and dependence which makes one want a friend, and try to find one in the Lord.

You are right, my precious boy, when you seek after the Lord, in humility and earnest supplication for His spirit to help you, not only before engaging in open air meetings, but in performing any duty. Always be humble, and get as near to the Lord as you can. What I mean by that is this: try to live so that you shall be worthy of the good Father's blessing and help. Never boast of your own strength. Never allow yourself to feel that you can do without God's precious care and protection.

Your disposition is very much like my own. My greatest difficulty has been to guard my temper, to keep cool in the moment of excitement or trial. I have always been too quick to resent a wrong, too impatient, or hasty. I hope you will be very careful, my son, on these points. He who can govern himself is greater than he who ruleth a city.

O, God bless my boys, and give them wisdom, faith and patience, and the living witness of Thy Spirit. O, keep them from all harm, shield them from temptation and sin.

Help them to *do right*, to act prudent, exemplary, and charitably, and make them valiant for Thy truth. This is my constant prayer for *you*, one and all. We are all usually well.

Contentment

Willard R., who had been sent to the relatively difficult field in Norway, expressed satisfaction with his assignment, which gratified his father.

June 13, 1905

I am pleased to learn that you are satisfied with your field of labor, and that you feel contented. It is a good thing for one who is on a mission, at least, to cultivate the feeling and habit of contentment. You know the story of the "old lady," who struggled for twenty years to get a contented mind and failed, until she concluded to be contented without it. Always make the best of everything.

Indifference

Alvin F. found Londoners indifferent to the gospel message he had come to share. Though an improvement over the sometimes violent opposition Joseph Fielding had encountered in England, the spirit Alvin F. found was not encouraging. Joseph F. remarked that "the world" has always been indifferent or hostile to the gospel of salvation, for it involves sacrifice and righteousness.

June 30, 1905

The great indifference of people generally to the gospel is an unmistakable evidence that the vintage time is either past or has not yet come, and now is the gleaning time. The hatred of the people toward us is due to dense ignorance mostly, and to some extent to willful malice.

They would rather accept slander than truth. But it is just as the Savior said to his ancient disciples, "Behold I send you forth as sheep in the midst of wolves. Be ye therefore wise as serpents and harmless as doves." Matthew 10:16-22. "And ye shall be hated of all men for my name's sake, but he that endureth to the end shall be saved." It is not so very different now than it was in the days of the Son of God. And if the world hated him and put him to death and his disciples, so will they hate *us*, for we are on the self same mission and business that they were on—the redemption and salvation of mankind. But the world loves pleasure more than God, and sin more than self-denial and righteousness.

The Rock

Matthew 16:17-18 has always been an important missionary text. The Church of England, like the Roman Catholic Church, interpreted the "rock" on which the church was to be built as being Peter, and believed the Lord's promise that "the gates of hell shall not prevail against it" was proof that the Lord had guaranteed an unbroken continuity of divine authority to the present time. Among the Latter-day Saint missionaries there seemed to be some question as to whether "the rock" referred to revelation or Christ. Joseph F. explained this controversial passage to H. Chase.

July 14, 1905

You ask this question: "Matthew 16:17-18. Does the 'rock' here referred to, mean revelation or Christ, or both?" It means both. The question was, "Whom do men say that I am?" The answer was "Thou art the Christ, the Son of the living God." The response was, "blessed art thou Peter, for flesh and blood hath not *revealed* it unto thee, but my Father who is in heaven." It was God who revealed to Simon or Peter that Jesus was *The Christ, The Son of the Living God."*

Now then, it was a revelation from God that made known to mankind, "The Christ," &c. And these two things constituted "The Rock" on which Christ's Church was to be built. Revelation alone is not sufficient. Christ alone would not suffice, for without Revelation from God, men, the world, could not know Christ, but they would still say, as of old, "he is John the Baptist, or 'Elias' or 'Jeremias,' or 'one of the prophets,' or perchance, he is 'Beelzubub,' or a 'deceiver,' &c. &c. But Revelation from God, not only identifies the fact that Jesus is "The Christ, The Son of the Living God," but also that "other foundation can no man lay than that [which] is laid, which is Jesus Christ." I Cor. 3:11. And further, that, "the stone which the builders rejected, the same is become the head of the corner." Matt. 21:42. And also see Ephes. 2:20. "And this is life eternal that they might know thee, the only true God and Jesus Christ whom thou hast sent." John 17:3. The grand object of Revelation is that Christ shall be made known to man, and that man knowing Him, and "the only true God" who sent Him, might through obedience obtain "life eternal." On the foundation of "Christ, The Son of the Living God," and "Revelation from God," is built His church and while the church so remains, "built" and building upon "this rock," the "gates of hell cannot prevail against it."

In a letter to George C., Joseph F. added:

Some have held that *revelation* alone was the "Rock" referred to. This could not be, because without Christ, revelation would not avail. Some have held it was "Christ alone" that was meant as the "Rock"; but this could not be, because without revelation, not even Simon Bar-jona could *know* that Jesus was "The Christ, the Son of the Living God," for "flesh and blood" not only *did not*, but absolutely cannot reveal Christ unto man. The revelation must come from God. Therefore, it may be summed up, that "The Christ," and "Revelation from God" constitute the "Rock" on which Christ built and will build His Church. . . . I know that both Christ and revelation are essential to the salvation of man, and indispensible to the building up of the Church. Both go together; they are inseparable, and one without the other would not avail.

Mercy

At this time, missionaries were often called upon to assume leadership roles in mission branches and conferences. Consequently, Alvin F. became involved in the case of a member who had been found guilty of serious transgression. Joseph F. touched upon the importance of upholding standards while extending mercy and charity to the truly repentant.

July 22, 1905

I was pleased with your letter in every way. You write a beautiful hand, and I approve the generous spirit manifested in it. With reference to the man A____. I have only to say we often have to use greater rigor in matters of that kind than would seem charitable, to avoid the chance for others to take liberties. But in all cases where charity can cover as a mantle a sin, or even a multitude of sins without harm accruing to others, the mantle of charity is the right thing. Your grandfather [Hyrum Smith] won the title of a "merciful man." No man will go farther than I to forgive a truly repentant sinner. See I Corinthians 13:13. Always lean towards mercy, but remember there is no forgiveness or remission of sin without repentance.

Joseph F. Smith's Temperament

On one occasion, Alvin F. urged his father not to work

so hard and to secure the services of a stenographer to help with correspondence. George and Willard had helped out in the office before leaving on their missions. Hyrum M. was occupied with his duties as an Apostle, and Joseph Fielding "is giving his mind to Church history, and is becoming an able writer and well posted in his line. He sometimes helps me after regular duty and I call on him now more than ever." Alfred W. Peterson helped out now and then, but the President of the Church continued without permanent help with correspondence for some time.

This letter gives a rare glimpse into the "workaholic" temperament of Joseph F. Smith and George Q. Cannon.

August 10, 1905

In your letter of July 21st answering mine of June 30, you give me a good lecture on taking care of myself and of having a stenographer to assist me in writing my letters, &c. All of which I accept in the loveliest kindness. But my son, I never yet put upon another any burden I was not willing to carry myself. I never asked, never expected anybody else to carry my load or lighten my cares. I never worked with any man who worked longer hours than I did myself. President George Q. Cannon is the only man I ever met to whose capacity for endurance I had to bow, and he possessed one gift—a rare one, too—which I, unfortunately, do not possess. It was this, at night when the toil of the day was done and we laid ourselves down for rest, the moment his head pressed his pillow, he slept and snored, and snored and slept, while I would toss and roll and sigh for sleep and rest, but like the will of the wisp, it would mockingly dance before my o'er wrought nerves, and perhaps for hours when most I needed it, elude me. And then I never failed to hear or sense the slightest sound or stir. I have carried this nervous temperament for more then 66 years and still I live! But it is due to kind providence, and to the mercy and love of

God, and not due to any wisdom, caution or power of my own. I shall endure it until He says it is enough, and then I will give up. It seems to me I could endure anything, if only I could feel that all was well with those I love. To see my family true to me, to each other, united, kind, and non-complaining and acknowledging the hand of the Merciful Father in all things, oh! this would be, and is, the elixor of life to me. I could then meet the contempt and hatred of the world without a sigh. I cannot be a one horse man. My lot compels me to cope with ponderous things. The burden would be too heavy for me to bear alone. But I can do it easily with God and my family on my side!

Temperance

Joseph F. counseled Willard to avoid extremes in all forms, particularly in fasting, a principle frequently abused by over-zealous missionaries, and over-indulgence in mail from home.

August 12, 1905

Be careful not to overload your stomach after fasting, and try to avoid as far as possible, long continued fasting, as I believe it to be hurtful to the system. To fast one day once a month is all the Lord requires, and the extreme that some elders go to in fasting for one, two or three days together, is in my judgment not only hurtful, but entirely unnecessary. Do not permit yourself to be drawn into any manner of extreme. Temperate living, temperate habits, temperate exertion, temperance in all things, is virtually a command of God.

You say that your two weeks' mail consisted of 17 letters. I think this is rather an extreme for a young missionary. While the receipt of letters from home and friends may serve to pass a few hours pleasantly, I scarcely think so many of them in so short a time would be conducive to your speedy acquisition of the language. One of the principle admonitions given to me, when a boy, from my temporal guardian, President George A. Smith, was this: "Joseph, always make short speeches, short prayers and write short letters," to all of which I have not, I am sorry to say, strictly adhered.

Proselyting Methods

In Norway, it was common for missionaries to pass out tracts without disclosing their identity. Not willing to compromise his honesty, Willard asked his father if such methods were consistent with the gospel. Appreciative of his son's integrity and at the same time aware of the need to reach those whose first impulse would be to reject "Mormons," Joseph F. offered this advice:

August 12, 1905

I can see no harm whatever in offering to sell people books of the Church without announcing anything with respect to your standing, or calling, provided they do not ask the questions. If anyone asks you who you are, tell them you are a missionary, or an Elder of the Church of Jesus Christ of Latter-day Saints, and if they are satisfied with this information, and are willing to buy your books well and good. If they press you further and demand more explicit explanation, simply go straight forward till you confess the whole truth. Never deny the truth, but it is not necessary that it should be told at all times. [I Corinthians 9:22 and II Corinthians 12:16 are quoted.] It seems that Paul felt justified in his effort to save men, to use innocent guile even, for the accomplishment of that purpose. If you desire to get a cow to eat an onion, feed her potatoes or apples. One by one incidentally slip in an onion, and she may eat it; but if you offer her the onion first, she will perhaps refuse to take it and your apples too. The Lord has said, "Be ye wise as serpents and harmless as doves"; but there is nothing that can compensate for the loss of honesty or integrity to the truth, though as I said before, while you always tell the truth, the whole truth need not always be told.

Dealing with Rejection

As Joseph F. well knew, tracting missionaries are not always greeted warmly at the door. When Willard described one incident of verbal abuse, Joseph F. wrote that such mistreatment "can only be accounted for on the ground that they are brutishly ignorant, or perniciously wicked." However, he advised the missionary to be generous in his feelings toward such persons.

January 11, 1906

I would fain give them the benefit of the doubt, and say they were pitiously ignorant! Never mind, my son, for so they treated our Lord and Master, in whom there was no sin. And He, as I hope you will do also, cried out, in the agony of death on the cross, and in the plenitude of His wonderful mercy, "Father forgive them for they know not what they do!" It is easy for me to forgive those who mistreat *me*, but it is *not so easy* to forgive those who would mistreat my boy. I like the manly spirit of your letter and the charity it expresses. But I pray you be wise and careful not to put yourself in the way of harm any more than you cannot help. As much as possible, go two and two as the disciples of old were commanded, to protect each other.

Right Hand or Left?

Alvin F. wrote to ask if there were a rule about pouring the oil with the right hand when administering to the sick. Answering the question, Joseph F. took occasion to warn his son against excessive attention to details that tend to obscure the true meaning of the ordinances.

December 16, 1905

The question you ask about anointing seems very simple to me. I think it is the general practice to pour the oil with the right hand. I suppose because most people are right-handed. But there is no law or rule against anointing . . . with the left. We shake with the right hand. In the endowments the signs and tokens are made and given with the right hand. When we lay but one hand on the sick it should be the right. We take the Sacrament with the right hand. The practice makes the rule. But always remember that it is not the rule, or practice, which gives life or force, but the true spirit. There is no good in splitting hairs nor in tickey-technical rules. "The letter killeth, but the Spirit giveth life."

Short Sermons and Sight-Seeing

Joseph F. counseled brevity in sermons and letters, and, while he recognized the value of sight-seeing, he advised his children to put duty first, as in this letter to George C.

February 17, 1906

You say, "In our meeting last night I spoke to the people for an hour and a half. I took for my text, Ephesians 4th., 5th verse and showed that Abraham's, Isaac's and Jacob's God was Paul's God, Christ's Father, and our God, and the only true One, and showed His character, etc." Of course, relying upon the Scriptures, all this seems to be very plain; but don't you think, George, an hour and a half is going it a little too strong? No matter how often, but be sure never permit yourself to become tedious. I am

decidedly pleased with the spirit of your letters, and hope
that you may always maintain the same. I am very glad
that you concluded not to accompany President Matson
on his journey to Rotterdam. I think it is better for you
all to remain carefully in your fields of labor, attending to
your legitimate duties as you may be called upon until your
missions are fulfilled, and when you obtain your honorable
release to return home, by the help of the Lord I will assist
you what I can to visit some of the most prominent cities
and places of interest convenient on your journey
homeward. But I would dislike very much to have the idea
go out that my boys were sight-seeing while on their
missions instead of attending to their regular duty. I say
always attend to our duties first and take all the pleasure
we can in the performance of them, and then trust to
Providence for the pleasures to come after.

Politics

Joseph F. Smith was a well-known and sometimes outspoken Republican. Elder Charles W. Penrose, president
of the European Mission in Liverpool during H. Chase's
mission was equally well known and outspoken as a Democrat. Thus, when the Republicans won the election of 1906,
Joseph F. counseled Chase to be sensitive of his mission
president's feelings, noting that partisan politics should not
become so entrenched as to divide brethren in the gospel.
Indicative of his own behavior in such matters, Joseph F.
later selected Elder Penrose to be one of his counselors in
the First Presidency.

December 14, 1906

Do not forget that Brother Penrose is a very sensitive
Democrat, and his political corns are awful sensitive and
tender. I would hate to feel like some of my Democratic
brethren feel. I try to keep my politics near the *surface*.
It is bad for them to "strike in."

94

The Constructive Approach

During the Christmas season, Alvin F. wrote home criticizing various holiday traditions in the different churches. They impressed him as contrary to the true spirit of Christmas. Though Joseph F. also found the celebrations inappropriate, he counseled Alvin to remember that his mission was not to criticize but to convert.

January 15, 1907

It will not do for us, in our capacity of missionaries to so attack sectarianism. We should portray the beautiful gospel building, restored anew to mankind, and invite them kindly to enter it, and leave them to discover by comparison the rapidly crumbling, tottering structure they now inhabit. Honey will capture more *flies* than vinegar, and will hold them faster when captured. Our mission is to save, not destroy; to build up, not pull down; to win by love, not coerce by fear or threats.

Selling Books

Not all proselyting success can be measured in baptisms, for contacts made and discussions held often prove productive later when the interest has had an opportunity to mature. Literature distributed may eventually reach someone who will be challenged and prepared to receive the missionaries. Such "planting" efforts are important for those who follow later to "harvest." But, as Joseph F. pointed out to George C., a missionary must never lose sight of his primary calling—to reach *people*, not merely distribute literature.

January 16, 1907

I am glad to note the renewed and increased diligence

of the elders in your conference, as reported in your letter. It is doubtless a good thing to distribute tracts, to sell books, to hold meetings, and conversations, &c. &c. This would indicate more or less activity and energy on the part of the elders, but in all such reports we learn very little about the results of sowing the seed. . . . While I was in England and Holland, the only thing I heard . . . was the marvelous figures showing the number of tracts &c. &c. sold, loaned and given away. All of which was good in its place, and I am not disparaging it in the least, but it seems to me the paramount object is to reach the hearts, sympathies, and friendship of the people, rather than the quantity of literature scattered; and the mere distribution of tracts &c. is not sufficient to gain the confidence and secure the affections of good people and remove prejudice and ignorance from the foolish.

Early to Bed

Nearing the end of his mission, George C. became intently involved in his work. Long hours were also demanded of President Smith, who nevertheless recognized the need for sufficient sleep and encouraged his son to be mindful of sensible, healthful routines.

February 17, 1907

You were writing your letter of January 8 after 12 midnight, and you had not "been to bed before 12 midnight for almost a month." I think I might almost say the same of myself. But whether it is I or you, it is all wrong! I know that in this respect I am guilty of transgressing the laws of life and health, and yet it seems as tho' I was impelled by necessity to do it. All day I give my time and effort to public duty, and what I have to do for myself and my *five* families I must do after working hours. Besides these duties necessary to myself and family, I do all the

writing, reading, reviewing of matter for the [*Deseret News*]
press, which I have to do by electric light, generally after
everybody except myself (not even excepting the office
guard), are wrapped in the arms of Morpheus. Still it is
wrong, especially is it not wise when necessity compels one
to get up early in the morning after working past midnight.
It is wrong even though one sleeps in the morning to make
up for lost rest, for it is turning day into night and night
into day. In a manner it is consuming artificial light at
much cost to the pocket and wasting free natural light,
also at more or less cost to health. . . .

The Lord said, "Retire to bed early," and this is wise
advice, but we do not heed it. Now let me say, Let us go to
bed early, that we may rise early and be refreshed. So far
as we can. It is God's plan. He tells us to do it, and we
should obey.

Promises and Sacrifice

Realizing he had been somewhat negligent in writing
home, Willard R. expressed his regrets and *promised* to
communicate more frequently. Joseph F. noted it is not
necessary to make promises. Quietly reforming, without
the danger of making promises that cannot be kept, will
suffice.

Willard also expressed gratitude for the sacrifices his
family had made to support him on his mission. Joseph F.
responded, putting in perspective the monetary expenses
and the eternal returns.

February 17, 1907

Do not make any more promises than you will surely
fulfill. You say you will write oftener &c. Never mind the
promise—do not make any and then you will not break
any! Two or three promises, if not carefully kept, will go
farther towards ruining one's character than months of

reticence. If you will only *keep well* and do your duty, I will ask no pledges.

You speak, my precious boy, of the "sacrifice" I am making in providing for my boys and for my family &c. &c. Do you know what "sacrifice" means? Let me tell you. If after all I am doing or can do for the welfare and happiness of my loved ones, they should turn their backs upon me, should deny the Faith, go to the bad, or bring disgrace or sorrow upon themselves or me or my family, then indeed would my labor of love become a sacrifice. But if my children will continue to love me, be true to themselves and therefore to me and to our God, O! then there is no sacrifice tho' it cost my all of worldly things and my life to boot. It will be all gain, all profit, all reward! I am living for my own salvation now and hereafter. Next to my own comes that of my children and their beloved and precious mothers. Nothing that I *can* do in the world that will secure this glorious end can be called a sacrifice. It is a labor of love, an aim for life eternal and the fulness of joy. "He that hath eternal life is rich." Eternal life is the greatest gift of God.

Always do your best, my son. Hearken to the voice of the good spirit. Keep yourself unspotted from the world. Shun secret vices, as you would shun the deadliest poison; and neither you nor I can make any sacrifice, though our effort to win the great prize, "eternal life," should cost us all we have of this world. My darling boy, I mean what I say and I am not over-drawing the facts. God my Father, bless you always and keep you pure and free. Mamma and all at home are well.

E. Wesley, Franklin R., C. Coulson, Calvin, Andrew K., and Hyrum M. (1907-16)

For eighteen of the last twenty-three years of his life, Joseph F. supported sons in the mission field. On February 21, 1907, the day after the Senate voted to seat Reed Smoot, Julina's son Elias Wesley left for his mission to Hawaii. Wesley had been born in 1886 at Laie, Oahu while Joseph F. and Julina were on the "underground." His appointment to some of Joseph F.'s former mission areas brought much satisfaction to his father, who enjoyed reminiscing about his Hawaiian days. After more than three years on the islands, Wesley was taken ill with typhoid and returned to Utah. A few years later, he was again called to Hawaii, this time as mission president.

While Wesley was serving his first mission to Hawaii, Franklin Richards, son of Sarah, was called to Great Britain. He served from October 1908 to February 1911 in Birkenhead, Preston, and Leyland.

On April 16, 1909, Charles Coulson (son of Alice) married Manon Lyman. Four days later they were on their way to Hawaii as missionaries. Manon served in the local MIA and assisted her missionary husband, later giving birth to their first child in the islands. They returned in 1911, just as another barrage of anti-Mormon articles began appearing in the nation's press.

A few months later, Joseph Fielding Smith, Jr., was sustained as a member of the Council of Twelve Apostles at the April conference, 1910. Calvin (son of Mary) accepted a call to the Swiss-German mission. Arriving in September 1910, he served in Freiberg, Werdau, Chemnitz, and Hamburg, Germany; and Zurich, Switzerland before returning in February 1913.

Shortly after Coulson and Manon returned from Hawaii, Andrew Kimball (son of Alice) was sent to Calvin's mission. Andrew served in Saxony, Zurich, Leipzig, and Königsberg from October 1911 to February 1914.

Finally, Hyrum M. was called to preside over the European mission in 1913. When World War I broke out, acting on his father's instructions, Hyrum evacuated the missionaries from all belligerent nations to neutral countries. He remained at his post until released in 1916.

In March 1915, Joseph F.'s wife Sarah passed away. Partly to assuage his grief, he took a trip to Hawaii, where in May he felt inspired to dedicate a temple site at Laie.

Sailing Experiences

Soon after he arrived in Hawaii, Wesley sent home photographs of himself and his companions on board the sailing ship that took them to their mission. The pictures reminded Joseph F. of tricks he had seen sailing crews play on unsuspecting passengers.

May 12, 1907

I suppose it is you away up in the rigging. On the Atlantic Ocean, if a "land lubber" goes up the rigging like that, the sailors follow him with cords and lash him to the rigging until he agrees to "treat" them, i.e., the whole crew. You had better look out what you do and where you go on shipboard. It is a rule among sailors, when a "green" passenger goes out onto the "forecastle," or *bow* of the ship, to draw a chalk line or mark behind him which he must not cross, until he shells out for the crew, i.e., until he "treats." There is nothing that pleases a sailor so much as to catch a minister on forbidden boards in the ship, so that they can make him "shell out" or back down. In the latter case they regard him as a "sky-pilot" of small caliber. Don't you let them play any tricks on you.

Death of a Daughter and Infant

On December 23, 1907, Joseph F.'s daughter Leonora Nelson passed away at the age of thirty-six, having given birth a few days previous to a stillborn daughter. She left a husband and five children and was the fifth child of Joseph F. and Mary Taylor Schwartz Smith to die at an early age. Joseph F. was nearly overcome with grief. Only the assurance of her righteous life on earth and well-deserved reward in the next life could comfort him. This tribute, written to Wesley, expresses both the grief at the loss of one so loved and the joy in the life of one so worthy that Joseph F. felt at the passing of his beloved Leonora.

December 27, 1907

Before this reaches you, through Ina's letter, you will have learned the sad and mournful tidings of our darling Leonora's death. It has been to me one of the severest blows I ever felt. It was so sudden and so unexpected that the first knowledge I received of it stunned me beyond measure.

On Tuesday the 17th inst. she gave birth to a pretty little girl, but it was lifeless when it was born. This was a sad, sad loss to her, and filled us all with sorrow. We buried the little baby on the 18th and we thought dear Nonie was getting along favorably. So sure were we that she was doing nicely, that I did not go to see her after the baby was buried, but contented ourselves with occasional enquiries over the telephone.

On Saturday the 21st I went to Cache Valley to attend

the Hyrum Stake conference. Spent Sunday 22nd at Wellsville in conference in the large new meeting house. Monday, 23rd, the Prophet's birthday anniversary, I started home on the Cache Valley train, reaching the City a little after noon. I was met at the station by a friend with the death-laden message that our darling Nonie had left us that morning for a better world. This terrible news almost stifled me. I felt dazed with astonishment and grief. I could not speak to anyone nor get relief from the crushing weight in my heart, until I reached the house, where on seeing Mamma and the children the fountain of my tears broke loose; for once I felt grateful for tears. And still it did not seem possible that our Nonie was gone. I drove at once to her home, and there indeed I found it was all too true! The scene I witnessed was heart-rending. We were all overwhelmed with grief. The little boys were crying and calling for their darling Mamma, and I cried for her too, but for the first time in her precious, lovely life she did not heed our cries nor answer to our calls.

Oh! my precious boy, there never has been and will never be to us but *one Nonie*! She was a Saint indeed. Her soul was all and only good. No murmurs, no complaints ever passed her lips. Her heart was full of kindness and her soul overflowed with love. If she ever spoke an unkind word of any living being, I never heard of it. She was patient in sickness, and in no case ever found fault. She was one of the best daughters that ever lived. She could not have been better. She was affectionate to her parents and loved them with all her heart. She loved her brothers and sisters, her aunts and her husband and her children. She was bright and intelligent, a good scholar and reader. The best of neighbors and the truest of friends. I never felt anything but the sweetest joy, happiness and satisfaction in her whole precious life. Everybody who knew her loved her, not only so, but admired and honored her.

I feel that she was perfect, as mortal being can be, as daughter, wife, mother and woman!

She loved the Lord and her religion and was true to them to her last breath. She was a pure-minded, white-souled angelic spirit, one out of a thousand. But few people really knew her!

Now, my son, I have shed tears for her loss to me, for her precious, sorrowing, heart-broken mother and sisters, and for her darling little motherless babes, until the fountain of my tears has well nigh dried up. And yet I know that all things are well with her. We do not mourn for her. We only have joy in her. We are all the better for her life's example, and the world is indebted to her for the glorious, shining path she graced by her presence in it. She has left here five lovely children, four boys and a girl. All perfect in mind and limb and joint, and beautiful.

No! we do not weep nor mourn for *her*. It is for our bereavement, our loss of her for time, that we grieve. We do not mourn as those without hope. We know we shall meet her again, where pain and sickness, death and sorrow will not come again, and where life and love and joy will ever reign. I cannot but feel that my own angel mother, and her own loved mother's mother were nearby with open arms and heavenly love to meet, receive and welcome her to their blessed abode, the paradise of God and the just, "a place of happiness, of rest, of peace, where they rest from all troubles and from all care. (See B. of M., Alma 40, also Alma 11:40-45.) God bless you my boy and comfort you. Be brave and true. Be faithful in your mission. Keep yourself pure and unspotted from the world. God lives. He does all things well. He knows best. He loved Nonie, for she was pure and good. All send love to you.

Redundancy

As Joseph F. had encouraged Wesley's older brothers

to brevity and clarity in their letters, he counseled Wesley to avoid redundancy in an effort to improve the quality of his expression.

April 10, 1908

Let me remind you that "loving and affectionate" are two words with almost the same meaning. Beware of tautology. Loving and true, or loving and faithful, or faithful and affectionate, or true and affectionate, are all right. You do not want to say "your loving and loving son," or "your affectionate and affectionate son," which "loving and affectionate" mean.

Leadership Responsibilities

In April, Wesley was called to preside over the Hilo conference, a position his father had held more than fifty years before. Joseph F. reflected on his Hawaiian experience and offered advice on the responsibilities of leadership.

April 10, 1908

Your letter from Laie, April 7 was duly received April 18th. I am glad you were honored with a re-appointment to Hilo, and to preside. The responsibility is a little greater, but it is a responsibility that develops experience and character. "The Lord and any one good man is a big majority." Keep close to the Lord in your conduct, and always be humble and unpretentious, and the Lord will bless you. I was placed to preside over the whole Island of Maui when I was much younger than you are now. I only did my best, leaving the rest with the Lord.

Later I was appointed to preside over Northern Hawaii, including Hamakua and Hilo and Kohala. I simply tried to do my best, and truly the Lord helped and blessed me. Several of those who were appointed to labor with me were much older than I was. Among them William W. Cluff, George Spiers, John Brown, and only the Lord made me equal to my tasks. It is true I readily learned the language, and not one got ahead of me in that. Keep your eyes open and be sure you are in good fellowship with the Lord. . . .

One thing I wish to impress upon your mind—i.e., (id est, or that is), in handling church funds or money not your own, be sure to keep a strict account of it, so that you can make an accounting of every cent of it, in a legitimate way. Be very careful not to use any money entrusted to your care for any purpose whatever, except for its legitimate purpose.

Perseverance

Times of discouragement came to Wesley, as they do to every missionary. Joseph F. understood that frustration and disappointment were part of the mission experience and encouraged his son to persevere, adding a few miscellaneous admonitions to better prepare him for the challenges of missionary work.

October 18, 1908

True, as you say, "If it were not the Lord's work, that we are engaged in" and if we were not mighty sure of it, we would all "feel like quitting." But the Lord does not love "quitters." Quitters never win; the battle is not to the strong, nor the race to the swift, but to him that endureth to the end. We are in it for life, and as life never ends we're in it for a long time; and the best of it is, we only begin in this life, and we don't propose to end it at all while life or thought or being lasts, or immortality endures. So make your mind up for a long and a strong fight, and a glorious triumph bye and bye. . . .

I am glad you like the natives and entreat them kindly. Love begets love, and kindness, kindness. One can scarcely expect to reap what he does not sow. Win the confidence of all men by uprightness, in walk and conversation. Always speak the truth and stand by it; never prevaricate, or dodge a responsibility and you will be known in your true light as a soul of honor.

A Sacred Calling

Shortly after Franklin R. left on his mission to England, his father wrote him a thoughtful letter drawing Franklin's attention to the sacred calling he had received, the high standards he was expected to maintain, and the impact his life had on his family.

October 18, 1908

I want you to bear in mind that the mission that you are going out upon is a very sacred matter, that it will not admit of any conduct on the part of any missionary that would not be becoming and respectful, and notwithstanding your youth, and inexperience in the world, I expect you to conduct yourself as a gentleman, courageous and respectful to all men, and above reproach. Let no man have it in his power to point at you justly the finger of scorn. Maintain the standard of truth and honor, no matter where you are, nor the character of any companion in which your lot is cast. Do not indulge in any practice that would be undignified or reprehensible. Remember your prayers and never be ashamed of your religion, nor of your people, and uphold the honor of the name you bear; be careful of your means and as I told you before you left home, never engage in any games of chance and do not condescend to vulgar joking or disrespectful language of any kind, nor engage with anybody in playing tricks upon your associates or anybody else. . . .

106

Remember that your grandfathers, Hyrum Smith and Willard Richards were among the founders under God, of the great latter-day work, and although both of them were not immediately martyred for the truth's sake, the lives of both of them were often in jeopardy for the test which they bore. You bear their names; for their sake and my sake and your own, and for the sake of the happiness of your precious mother and all my family, hold sacred in your keeping their honor. Remember, my son, that I was left an orphan at the age of six years; that I suffered with a widowed mother the hardships and persecutions incident to the martyrdom of the Prophet and your grandfather Hyrum Smith, and of the frontier life of a pioneer to help to establish the Church of Jesus Christ of Latter-day Saints in the world. And nothing could grieve me worse than to have one of my boys turn traitor to the cause of Zion, or deny the faith. Pure and upright men, men who are honest and deal justly are never among those who fall away from the truth and turn enemies to the cause of Zion. I want you to be humble and prayerful, for "pride always goes before destruction, and a haughty spirit before a fall."

Avoiding Contention

Knowing that Franklin R. would encounter men and women whose hostility to the Restoration might go beyond reason, Joseph F. counseled forbearance and urged his son to avoid contention whenever possible.

November 23, 1908

Those who are most bitter and wicked in their hearts toward the gospel, and toward the Church are, as a rule, the most ignorant and corrupt. Now and then a naturally good person may be blinded with prejudice thro' ignorance and misunderstand, but such will not be vicious or vindictive. Such persons may be reached thro' kindness and perseverance.

Of one thing be sure. There is no use to argue or contend with a truly wicked, corrupt person. It would be time lost. Never *contend* anyway. Try to set forth *reasons* and good thoughts and gospel truths, but don't contend. Be careful not to provoke argument or contention either with "saint or sinner." Avoid it. Remember the admonition of the Savior to his disciples, "Let your communications be yea, yea or nay, nay, for whatsoever is more than these cometh of evil."

Miscellaneous Admonitions

Try to learn by study and by ear. Be a good listener, and remember every good thing you hear. Keep a diary, and note down good things to refer to afterward, to refresh your mind. Do not write long letters. Write briefly and oftener if necessary. Postage is cheap now between England and here. I want you to be sociable with those who preside over you. Do not shun nor avoid them, nor keep anything hidden from them. Conduct yourself so that you will have no secrets to keep from them. Be open-hearted, frank and honest toward God and man. And above all things do not compromise yourself with any woman or girl. One of the most deadly sins known is the sin against virtue. Keep yourself pure and unspotted from the world.

Traits of an Effective Missionary

December 27, 1908

My Dear Son Franklin:

Your very interesting letter of December 7, reached me on the 23rd inst., and I read it with deep interest and pleasure in the thought that you are shaping yourself for the labors of the mission in very good form. The very best element for successful missionary labor is humility, coupled with persistence and a determination to do one's whole duty. In order to do this one must be careful not to divide his attentions too much with other things. You have started in to win, and victory will depend upon your integrity to the work you have begun. It will be time enough after you have completed your mission and received an honorable discharge to relax your mind by turning your thoughts into other channels. And yet I sincerely hope that you will never dismiss from your mind an earnest desire to help to build up Zion and live and spread the truth restored to earth through Joseph Smith the Prophet throughout all the rest of your days. Please remember, Frankie, that nothing can compare with honesty, pure and simple in thought and deeds in anything that you undertake. And above all things one must be honest and sincere in the performance of his religious duties. On these lines we are dealing with our conscience and with our God, but in every phase of life strict honesty is the "best policy." Do not forget the Lord and He will not forget you, and you will have claim upon Him for the blessings you most need. When you pray ask for what you need, without a multiplicity of words. We are never heard in our prayers for "much speaking." Do not indulge in too much fun-making, in playing jokes, or unfriendly criticism. In fact, observe the golden rule, "Do unto others as you would like to be done by." . . . You are sent out to teach the truth and to live the truth.

Expressions of Contentment

Joseph F. was gratified to receive a letter from Wesley expressing contentment with his calling. He told Wesley how pleased he was with his attitude. He then cautioned Wesley about making too frequent expression of a righteous feeling, lest it create feelings of self-righteousness.

June 17, 1909

Your very welcome letter of May 4th from Waimea, came to hand on May 24th, the first pages of which was written in Hawaiian and I am very pleased to note that you have made very good improvement in the language since your first attempts to write in the Hawaiian language. I am very glad that you are satisfied with your field of labor. You say, "I am perfectly satisfied and contented with my calling, never have I felt better. Home is the least of my troubles, for I have no desire whatever to return before the proper time. I don't want anybody to interfere with my mission, my mind is made up to remain here just as long as the Priesthood wishes to keep me, and I am going to try hard to do my duty all the time. My appointment could not have been better. I would rather be here than in Honolulu by a long margin. But I am willing to go and do everything that the Spirit of the Lord wishes me to do. And I will be happy all the time, for my faith is in him and I know he will call me where I am needed."

I have quoted the above from your letter and I commend it very highly and congratulate you, my son, on possessing the feeling expressed therein, and while I hope you will continue to possess the same feeling and spirit until it shall be said *enough,* I do not think it will be necessary for you to repeat the language very often, lest someone will think that you are either parading your virtue or merely talking to hide a suspected desire to the effect that your mission could not end too soon to suit you. Of course, I believe just what you say, and I shall take it for granted that inasmuch as you mean it, you will be true to the sentiment without ever blowing a trumpet about it. I hope you will take this in the spirit in which I intend it, for I have confidence in you and it doesn't matter what you say or how you say it, I shall always believe you are honest in your expressions, but others might put a different construction on your real meaning by often repeating it.

Discretion

When Wesley reported unfavorable impressions of his mission president, Joseph F. responded by challenging not his son's observations, but his wisdom in expressing such critical remarks. Even strictly honest reports need not always be broadcast.

June 17, 1909

In your letter to Mamma of a recent date, you spoke considerably of President W____. You should be very careful about writing sentiments relative to the doings or character of any individual and more especially about your presiding officer. The Prophet Joseph Smith laid down the following rule, "Never permit yourself to write down on paper anything that you would not like to have made public." Of course, when you do speak or write, tell the truth, but you know it is said, even the truth should not be said at all times. It is not lying, nor deceitful, nor is it likely to injure anyone to withhold from speaking unpleasant truths. And be careful never to attempt the difficult task of telling all you know.

Living in the Present

As the end of Wesley's mission neared, Joseph F. was concerned that he not lose sight of his calling and begin to anticipate returning home. He reminded Wesley to live in the present and let the future take care of itself.

June 17, 1909

Your welcome letter of June 3rd reached me on the 16th inst. written from Lihue, again you repeat that so far, your new field of labor has been very good and your treatment by the natives has been of the best. You say your friends are many and you believe with the help of the Lord you will be able to do some good while on that island, that the people seem to be pleased to see you and you are as much pleased to see them; so that you feel that your stay there will prove to be a very pleasant one; that the time is fast flying by, this year will soon be gone, and another round placed in your ladder. Now, some folks might think the last sentence hinted very strongly toward the desire that the end might soon come looking for your release to come home. While I sympathize with you and realize that the desire is natural for you, or for anyone else to reach the end of a journey or a mission, it is not well to lay yourself open to the suspicion that you would like to hasten. No matter about the future, we live in the present, our duty is now, we can do nothing tomorrow, but only today. "Let the future take care of the future, life's troubles come never too late." Let your mind dwell on what you have done and not on what you expect to do, or are looking forward to.

Learning to Write

As Franklin's first letters began to arrive from the mission field, his father recognized many of the errors that characterized his first efforts at writing. He sympathized with Franklin's difficulties and, rather than criticize him directly, noted the similarities to his own first attempts. Important too, is Joseph F.'s readiness to acknowledge some dissatisfaction with his own expressive abilities.

August 12, 1909

Your very welcome letter of June 14th reached me on the 27th inst. I always read your letters with a great deal of interest. One thing that adds to the interest of your letters is that they remind me very much of the character of letters I myself used to write in the days of my boyhood.

It is true, I did not know very much about the proper use of words, and the proper application of them in trying to express my thoughts. In later years on looking over some of my earliest letters, they reminded me very much of a little bird just getting its feathers and beginning to learn to fly. The poor little bird makes a very poor out at the beginning in its attempts to soar aloft on its half-fledged wings, but it persists in trying until, at length, by means of full-fledged wings and experience in their use, it becomes master of the air. I have no doubt the little bird is much more entitled to credit for having accomplished its power of flight and perfect use of wings than I, for while I, alas, though still persisting in my effort to clothe the pinions of my thought in fitting words, find that I am still lacking in the accomplishment of my purpose, and I have come to the conclusion that the real object of language is to convey one's thoughts in the simplest form of speech, and not to befog or mystify or conceal one's meaning by a multiplication of similar terms or a superabundance of words. It is said of the great Disraeli, world-famed for his eloquence, that he used only the simplest words to convey his thoughts.

I hope that you, my son, AND I, will reach the point at which we may be able to say all that it is necessary for us to say in the simplest, plainest possible words.

A Father's Concern

Illness struck the Smith family several times in 1909. In July, daughter Donette underwent a serious operation; in September, Martha suffered an attack of appendicitis. Concern for his daughters and the strain of his duties gave Joseph F. a cold, and he wrote Hyrum M., "Yesterday I was so tired and shakey I do not know whether I spelt my own name right or wrong. You know I am not always a success as a spellist anyway."

In October, Joseph F.'s youngest child, Royal, was run

113

over by a horse and buggy "and was considerably bruised."
Martha's appendix was removed in November. Then came
news that Wesley had contracted typhoid fever in Kauai.
He was soon transferred to Honolulu, where Coulson and
Manon could nurse him back to health.

Thus, supporting three missionaries, helping Willard
financially to build a house, and paying doctor bills and a
surprisingly high property tax, Joseph F. wrote Franklin,
"I am about drained dry!" Nevertheless, as he made clear to
Coulson, his main concern was for the health and welfare
of his children.

December 13, 1909

I hope you will do all you can for [Wesley], and that
he follows the advice of the physician about eating. Good
fresh butter-milk, if it could be obtained, would be
wholesome for him. Typhoid fever is a disease of the
stomach and bowels, and it sometimes, if not always, leaves
the intestines in a most tender and delicate condition.
There is much danger of eating too much, and of eating
indigestible food, after the disease has spent itself and has
left its victim. So be careful that he does not eat too heartily
of hearty food for some time after the fever leaves him. I
wrote Manon on the 8th and sent you my cheque for $15,
and I wrote you on the 10th in acknowledgment of yours
of November 30, and sent you a dollar to help out a little
on Christmas.

My expenses for doctor bills and nurse bills and
hospital fees this year have been terrific. And my taxes,
which I have just finished paying have reach[ed] to more
than $1000, mostly for our homes from which we derive
no income but are a constant expense. Then there is my
winter's supply of coal for all my homes which is no
bagatelle with coal at $5.25 per ton. But these are the
least of my troubles in comparison to sickness. I do not
want Wesley to return to Kauai until he is perfectly sound

again. I shall anxiously await further word from either of
you. God bless my boys, and keep them from harm.

Harmony

When Franklin related a minor disagreement with his
mission president, Joseph F. took occasion to teach a lesson
about the importance of harmony among the missionaries
and their leaders.

February 19, 1910

I am sorry you were not a little more discreet in
speaking to President Penrose. Boys on missions should
cultivate amity with all, and more especially with their
file leaders and presidents. I hope you will keep on the
good side of President Penrose, and all of your
companions. Missionaries should all be as members of one
family and each should strive to make it pleasant for all
the rest. Strife, or differences, or any degree of the spirit
of disunion existing among them just so much weakens
their influence and impairs their usefulness and efficiency.
Avoid carefully giving offense to any, but always be ready
to show kindness and sympathy.

Love and Encouragement

On February 17, 1909, Manon gave birth to a baby girl.
Joseph F.'s wife Julina, a professional midwife, was in atten-
dance. The baby brought great joy to Coulson and Manon,
joy shared by Joseph F., as expressed in this letter to Manon.

October 5, 1910

I am glad you enjoy so much your dear little baby girl,
and I sincerely hope she will continue to enjoy good health

and grow and develop into a good girl who will take as much delight and have as much joy in her mother as her mother is experiencing in her. I like the spirit of your letter and hope you will continue to be buoyant in spirit, and hopeful and never yield to discouragement or obstacles that may be in your way. I hope you will succeed in winning over to duty the young people of Hilo, and that you will have pleasure in the accomplishment of that work. Of course, I am a little sorry that you feel so discouraged about learning the language, but I hope you will keep on trying as long as you shall remain there and get as much knowledge of the language as you can.

Power of the Gospel

Give my aloha nui to sister Napoleon and her husband, and to all the good Latter-day Saints at Hilo. And tell them for me that the gospel which they have embraced is the greatest thing that has ever been revealed from God to mankind, as it contains the fulness of the gospel of salvation for the living and for the dead and reaches the necessities of every soul, living or dead, in all ages of the world. It is, indeed, the power of God unto salvation.

Short Letters

Having been in the mission field only a couple of months, Calvin wrote long weekly letters to his mother, brothers, and sister. Joseph F. gently reminded his son that it is better not to write such long letters that take him away from his missionary duties.

November 11, 1910

I have before me four long interesting letters written by you on the following dates: September 22nd, and 30th, and October 7th, and 16th. All of which I was glad to receive and have read with very much pleasure and interest. I have also read your letters to Mamma and Samuel and James and also to Sister Lucy, all written within a very short period of time. While it is very interesting to get long letters from you, it must be considerable of a labor for you to write so many *long* letters and keep up with your other labors and duties in the field. I hope you will be prudent and not undertake to do too much, nor overdo yourself. It was a rule of your late kinsman, President George A. Smith, to make short prayers, but fervent ones, short sermons and to the point, and short letters well digested. It is often much more of a labor to write a short letter well composed and digested than a very lengthy rambling one. I think you are a very good letter writer, only that your hand writing appears rather small for so large a boy.

The Burdens of a Prophet

In his 73rd year, Joseph F. Smith was the object of a rash of scurrilous articles published in national magazines. Congress passed legislation aimed at curbing Mormon immigration and launched an investigation into the sugar industry, one of the Church's major business concerns. The issue of prohibition was being raised in Utah, and the Church was attacked both for being too involved and for not being involved at all. It was a trying time for the Church's aging President, as indicated in this letter to Calvin.

March 29, 1911

Our General Conference will begin one week from today. I look forward to it with considerable dread. Conference times are periods of great responsibility for me. I am not so young, nor so strong as I used to be, and the weight of increasing responsibilities wears upon me somewhat more than they did when I was more vigorous. But the Lord has given me strength, so far, to carry my portion of the burden, for which I am most grateful. I feel happy in the good reports from you and Andres [attending Brigham Young University]; and have reason to be proud and hopeful of my sons. Your brothers at home are all good men and boys, and are doing their duty so far as I know. Fielding was ordained a deacon last Sunday. . . .

I have written so few letters when the pen of late, I have almost forgotten how. But I have not forgotten how to sign my name. I do that from ten to two hundred and fifty times daily. I intend to send you and Andres $25 [their monthly allowances] each tomorrow. God bless my boy.

Mission Opportunity

Joseph F. was anxious that his sons make the best possible use of the mission opportunities, for the character traits developed and demonstrated during a mission are indicative of what may be expected throughout the rest of their lives. He urged Calvin to take advantage of every opportunity, as the time would pass quickly.

March 30, 1911

Two or three years is a very short time in which to reach all the people that a missionary should deliver the message of salvation to. A missionary only realizes the opportunities he has missed when it is too late. After your mission has been completed and you are preparing to return home, you will reflect upon the time you have spent in the field and wish you had improved your time even better than you did. At least this is the case with most of us.

The man who is devoted to his work and who is trying

118

to make the best of his time will plan his work so that he will have something to do all the time. When he is not out tracting or holding meetings he will be visiting the Saints or improving his mind by studying the scriptures and preparing himself to teach those who are in darkness in such a way that they will not be left in doubt when he explains the gospel to them, and they will know that he understands what he is trying to teach them, even if they cannot grasp the truth themselves.

Too many of our missionaries spend their time idly, sight-seeing or wandering around in the parks, attending theatres or places of amusement. This should not be. It is all right to go to the theatre once in a while, or to go out in the parks, where it is nice and cool, for recreation, but to lounge around idly during the day or sight-seeing and spending the time that should be devoted to missionary work is not right. Neither is it the proper thing for missionaries to sit up late at nights, and then stay in bed in the mornings when they should be planning the work to be done. Many of the Elders sleep away and idle away the best part of their lives when they should be up and hustling.

The elder who is devoted to his work, who is energetic and who puts his trust in the Lord and is dependent upon Him for his support, is the best missionary. The one who has all the money he desires and spends his time in idleness and sight-seeing and putting on airs with fashionable clothes and cane, who attends theatres when he should be visiting Saints or holding meetings or improving his time, will never be as happy and faithful as the boy who has to make the best of his time and means.

Tithing

Joseph F. explained to Andrew the principle of tithing as it relates to missionaries.

July 12, 1912

I pay my tithing on the means I send my boys. They do not need to tithe it again, but can do so if they desire to. One who is on a mission is not as a rule earning money, but souls. However, if he has an income from flocks, herds, farms, or stocks and bonds or rents, he should pay his tithing on any and all of these (and on gifts). An elder is not expected to give one tenth while on a mission, but the *whole* of his time and talent.

Duties of a Prophet Father

As President Smith grew older, the demands of his office increased. Time spent with his family gave him great joy, though it seemed hard to come by. He shared his perplexity with Andrew.

November 6, 1912

I often feel sorely condemned for not writing oftener to you and Calvin. But it is hard for me to do it, with all the rest I have to do. It is true I go to the theatre occasionally with the Mammas and children, but whenever I do I cannot help thinking the time would be better spent in writing to my boys or doing some other work. . . . But I have so little time to visit with my family, I try to reconcile my visits occasionally with my families with my duty.

Thoughtful Reading

Joseph F. sent a copy of a general conference report and several other booklets to Andrew. He encouraged him to read them carefully, so that the ideas of the Brethren, like memorized scriptures, might be internalized and become part of him, rather than just passing through his mind.

June 29, 1913

I hope . . . these little books will afford you some useful reading for missionary work, and I hope you will find time between the performances of your arduous duties to peruse them; and let me admonish you, my son, that casual and hasty reading is never as profitable as careful, thoughtful reading. Always weigh matters that you read carefully, and grasp or master the subject. That kind of reading is profitable; I realize, however, that it is not always possible to give proper study to the reading of books when one is crowded with continuous and important other duties, but as the reading of these books will be along the line of qualifying you the better for your mission work, if you have time to read them at all, you can afford to read them well. The reading of the scriptures is never so effective and therefore never so profitable as when the salient points of doctrine are committed to memory. A few good passages of scripture learned by heart are worth more than an entire reading of the Bible without an object in mind other than to read.

Death

In October 1915, Zina, Hyrum's sister, the daughter of Joseph F. and Edna Lambson, passed away. Only months before, Sarah Ellen Richards, Presidents Smith's second wife, had died, and the remorse was almost unbearable to President Smith. He wrote Hyrum and poured out his heart and soul in his grief.

November 3, 1915

I cannot yet dwell on the scenes of the recent past. Our hearts have been tried to the core. Not that the end of mortal life has come to two of the dearest souls on earth to me, so much as at the sufferings of our loved ones, which we were utterly powerless to relieve. Oh! How helpless is mortal man in the face of sickness unto death! We prayed and pled with all our souls for restoration and life, but our prayers and pleadings were in vain. Their times had come—that of my darling "Mamma" S. and my lovely baby girl! Oh! Why should it be? I do not blame the Lord, nor charge Him with being responsible, either for their sufferings or their death. I believe frail human strength and nature are more responsible for moral ailments and short lives than is the will, or the pleasure, or the purpose of God. And yet, we acknowledge the hand of God in that which is, or comes, because He suffers it to be. When we better understand the laws of nature, and of life and health, we will better comprehend the mysteries of pain, disease, and death. Even then, it will be hard to part from those around whom our very heart-strings are wrapped in deathless love! And this will, and should be, so, notwithstanding the glorious hope and assurance which the Gospel gives, that those who die in the Lord shall not taste of death. They are not dead, but live, and we shall meet them again and resume the joys of life and exaltation together beyond the grave, above the power or recurrence of death forever more. I thank God for my loved ones, both on this and on the other side of the veil of what men call death. With all my heart I love those yet here, and, if possible, the cords of love for those who have passed beyond grow stronger day by day. God bless you my son, together with your precious little flock.

Calamity

Difficulties in Europe began as Hyrum and his family arrived in England in 1914 for his second mission, this time as president of the European Mission. By 1916, a full-scale war was underway, and as overseer of the European missionaries, Hyrum had to locate and transfer missionaries in dangerous situations into nonviolent areas and to com-

122

municate with their loved ones as to their safety. During this period Hyrum was imprisoned in Germany as an English spy because his initials, HMS, indicated he was in the service of the Crown. After clarification, he was released unharmed. He also related in his diary accounts of the zeppelin attacks on England and the damage and loss of property and life. In receiving this information, his father wrote:

February 19, 1916

I trust and pray that you and all of our people may escape from the terrible raids of the zeppelins that are occasionally made on the defenseless cities and towns of Great Britain. It seems to me that the only object of such raids is the wanton and wicked destruction of property and the taking of defenseless lives. No such thing as that was ever known, so far as my understanding goes, in any so-called civilized country before the present time. It appears that the spirit of murder, the shedding of blood, not only of combatants, but of anyone connected with the enemy's country, seems to have taken possession of the people, or at least the ruling powers in Germany. What they gain by it, I do not know. It is hardly possible that they expect to intimidate the people by such actions, and it surely does not diminish the forces of the opposition. By such unnecessary and useless raids in the name of warfare, they are losing the respect of all the nations of the earth. Well, my son, we pray that you and all who are under your direction may escape from these calamities. Preach the Gospel, be faithful, teach the Elders and the Saints to put their faith and trust in the Lord, for indeed these are days of trouble and calamity which have been spoken of by the prophets, and it behooves all men to repent and to turn to the Lord before their day of repentance is past and destruction overtakes them.

Epilogue

Throughout his life, Joseph F. Smith prayed for the success and safety of the missionaries. When Joseph Fielding had been in the mission field for one month, Joseph F. wrote the following prayer, expressing his love and concern for his son and all who are called to missionary labors.

July 18, 1899

Our hearts are full of blessing for you and [Joseph] Richards . . . and together with all your companions we hold you up in remembrance before the Lord whenever we pray. O! God, my Father, bless, comfort, sustain and make efficient my sons, and all *thy* servants in the mission field. When doors are shut in their faces, give them grace, forbearance and forgiving hearts. When coldly spurned by scornful men, warm them by thy precious love; when cruelly treated and persecuted be *thou* present to shield them by thy power. Make thy servants to *know thou* art God, and to feel thy presence. Feed them with spiritual life and with perfect love which casteth out all fear and may all their bodily needs be supplied. Help them to store their minds with useful knowledge, and their memories to retain thy truth as a well filled treasure. May they be humble before *thee* and meek and lowly as thy glorious Son! Put their trust in *thee*, in thy word, and in thy gracious promises. And may wisdom and judgment, prudence and presence of mind, discretion, and charity, truth and purity, and honor and dignity characterize their ministry and clothe them as with holy garments. O, God, bless abundantly thy servants with every needed gift and grace, and holy thought, and power to become thy sons in very deed!! And thus we pray for you, and I have this assurance: If you will use good judgment, act wisely, and guard yourselves so far as possible from cunning men and deceitful women, and the wicked devices of the world, *all* will go well with you. And God will deliver you out of every snare and trouble and help you magnify his name and honor his cause and will bring you home in safety.

For eighty years Joseph F. Smith helped build the kingdom of God. From Nauvoo to the Great Salt Lake Valley, he learned from the prophets and counseled with them. He preached the gospel at home and abroad, and supported twelve sons on missions to foreign lands. He sat in counsel with four Presidents of the Church, beginning with Brigham Young, and, as President himself, presided over the Church in difficult times. He suffered the deaths of both parents at an early age, and throughout his life grieved for the loss of his own wives and children. But his faith in God and his testimony of the gospel never wavered.

In January 1918, his firstborn son, Hyrum, died of a ruptured appendix. Joseph F. was grief-stricken for days, to the point of exhaustion. Eight months later, Hyrum's wife Ida passed away, adding to his grief and further weakening him physically. Though he survived the influenza epidemic of 1918, as World War I drew to a close he contracted pneumonia. He died on November 19, 1918, having just marked his eightieth birthday.

Index

Index

Maui: Joseph F. assigned to, 5; temporal conditions on, 7; spiritual condition of, 8; Saints of, dissatisfied with leader, 20-21
Means, use of, 81
Meditation, need for time for, 15
Mercy, 88
Millennial Star, 18
Mining disaster, 36
Missionaries, traits of effective, 108-9
Missionary tool, Book of Mormon as, 69-70
Missionary work, 106-7, 118-19
Model of righteousness, 35-36
Molokai, 10
"Mormon Corridor," 4
Motherhood, 2, 34-35

Nahuna, 10
Nauvoo, 14
Nebeker, Perry, 51
Nelson, Leonora Smith (daughter), 101-3
Nibley, Charles W., 25, 78, 79
Nuttall, L. John, 23

Open air meetings, 16
Orphan boy, adoption of, 19

Parkinson, George C., 51
Partakers of sacrament, 72-74
Penrose, Charles W., 51, 78, 115
Perpetual Emigration Fund, 25
Perseverance, 105-6
Plays, Joseph F. sees, 17
Politics, 94
Power of gospel, 116
Praise, receiving, 66-67
Pratt, Lorus, 25-26
Pratt, Orson, 23, 25-26, 27
Pratt, Parley P., 4
Prayer: for son, 48-49, for missionaries, 125-26
Promise to son Joseph Fielding, 63-64
Promises, 97-98
Prophet, burdens of, 117-18, 120

Proselyting methods, 91-92
Prudence, 37, 40-42
Public speaking, fear of, 31

Quieting of opposing crowds, 16-17

Reading, 120-21
Receiving praise, 66-67
Redundancy, 103-4
Rejection, 92
Reorganized Church of Jesus Christ of Latter Day Saints, 14
Repentance, 9-10
Retiring early, 96-97
Rewards, 82-83
Rich, Charles C., 13-14, 18
Richards, Sarah Ellen: marriage of, 22; goes to England with Joseph F., 24; watches over ill son, 34-35; death of daughter of, 75-76; son of, sent to England, 99; death of, 100, 121-22
Richards, Willard, 22, 107
Right or left hand, 92-93
Roberts, B. H., 59, 65
Rock, the, 86-88

Sacrament, partakers of, 72-74
Sacred callings, 106-7
Sacrifice, 97-98
Safety in companionship, 64
Sailing experiences, 100-101
San Bernardino, 4
Sandwich Islands, 2-3
Satan and human weakness, 70-72
Schwartz, Mary Taylor, 29, 101
Selling books, 95-96
Self-control, 83-85
Sheffield district, 15, 17
Ship, mission purchases, 4
Short sermons, 93-94
Shurtliff, Louie, 59, 63-64
Sight-seeing, 93-94
Smith, Alexander, 14
Smith, Alice (Alibo) (daughter), 75-76
Smith, Alma L., 19-21
Smith, Alvin F. (son), 77-98

129

Index

self-control, 83-85; on
contentment, 85; on indifference,
85-86; on the "rock," 86-88;
on mercy, 88; on work habits,
88-89; on temperance, 90-91;
on proselyting methods, 91-92;
on dealing with rejection, 92;
on use of right or left hand,
92-93; on short sermons and
sight-seeing, 93-94; on politics,
94; on the constructive approach,
95; on selling books, 95-96; on
retiring early, 96-97; on
promises and sacrifice, 97-98;
death of wife Sarah, 100, 121-22;
on sailing experiences, 100-101;
on death of daughter Leonora,
101-3; on redundancy, 104; on
leadership responsibilities, 104-5;
on perseverance, 105-6; on
sacred nature of missionary work,
106-7; on traits of effective
missionary, 108-9; on
expressions of contentment,
109-10; on discretion, 111; on
living in present, 111-12;
expresses concern for health
of son, 114-15; on harmony,
115; on love and encouragement,
115-16; on power of gospel, 116;
on short letters, 116-17; on
burdens of presidency, 117-18,
120; on mission opportunities,
118-19; on tithing, 119-20; on
thoughtful reading, 120-21; on
death, 121-22; on war's
calamities, 123; prays for
missionaries, 125-26; death
of son Hyrum, Hyrum's wife,
and Joseph F., 126
Smith, Joseph Fielding (son), 59-75,
79, 99
Smith, Joseph Richards (Buddie)
(son), 24, 34, 59-75
Smith, Josephina ("Ina") Coolbrith
(cousin), 10
Smith, Levira (wife), 13, 19, 21, 22

Smith, Lovina (sister). *See* Walker,
Lovina Smith
Smith, Martha (daughter), 113-14
Smith, Martha Ann (sister), 1
Smith, Mary Fielding (mother), 1-2
Smith, Royal (son), 113-14
Smith, Samuel H. (uncle), 13
Smith, Samuel H. B. (cousin), 13,
23-24, 31
Smith, Sarah (half-sister), 1
Smith, Silas (cousin), 5, 12
Smith, Willard R. (son), 77-98
Smith, Zina (daughter), 121-22
Smoot, Reed, 77, 79
Snow, Lorenzo, 19-21, 59, 77
Speaking, fear of public, 31
Spiers, George, 105
Spirit, seeking the, 83-85
Statehood, efforts to gain, 30
Street meetings, 16, 83-84
Sullivan, Barry, 17

Taylor, John, 29, 30
Taylor, John W., 78
Teacher, thrashing of, 2
Temperament, 88-90
Temperance, 90-91
Territorial legislature, 22
Testimony: obtaining a, 60-62;
of servants of Lord, 65-66
Tithing, 119-20
Truth, discerning, 36

"Underground," on the, 29-30, 99
Unpleasant experiences, 80-81
Utah war, 12-13
Ute Indians, 3-4

Vaquaro, 4
Vocabulary, 18
Voice of warning, 65-66

Waimea, 110
Walker, Chief, 3-4
Walker, Lovina Smith (sister), 14
Warning, voice of, 65-66
Washington, General George, 47

131